YouMap®

●●●

Find Yourself. Blaze Your Path. Show the World!

A step-by-step guide to discover and land a job you'll love.

Kristin A. Sherry

Black Rose Writing | Texas

The final approval for this literary material is granted by the author.

First printing

Although the author and publisher have made every effort to ensure that the information in this book was correct at press time, the author and publisher do not assume and hereby disclaim any liability to any party for any loss, damage, or disruption caused by errors or omissions, whether such errors or omissions result from negligence, accident, or any other cause.

ISBN: 978-1-68433-143-7
PUBLISHED BY BLACK ROSE WRITING
www.blackrosewriting.com

Printed in the United States of America
Suggested Retail Price (SRP) $19.95

YouMap® is printed in Garamond
Edited by Beth Crosby
YouMap® logo design by Crystal Davies, Davies Designs

Praise for YouMap®

● ● ●

"We're all born without life and career instructions. For many it's a complicated puzzle whose pieces never seem to fit together the way we'd like, leaving us unhappy and discouraged. With *YouMap®* Kristin Sherry has created THE instruction manual for solving the puzzle and hitting the career bullseye. She's created a life-changing framework that uses science to design the art of the possible. Using her methodology I guarantee you will love yourself, your career, and yes, Mondays!"

KEN TASCH, Chairman & CEO, Richard Dudgeon, Inc. and author of *Business Brainfood: A Real-World Playbook for Business Mastery*

"YouMap is a gem. It reads as if Kristin Sherry is sitting right next to you, helping you to identify your personal strengths and to clearly see how you add value to others; then, it teaches you how to communicate that in the best way possible.

It's full of wisdom, yet remains--dare I say--downright fun to read.

Reading this book is like hiring a masterclass coach—and then benefiting from the coach's top-tier network. A brilliant storyteller, Kristin Sherry teaches us through one interesting, insightful, real-life example after another.

Regardless of your personality type, age, or current career path, I guarantee you'll find lessons in this book that will help you enjoy your work more—and make you better at what you do."

JUSTIN BARISO, popular Inc.com columnist and author of *EQ Applied*

"I usually struggle to enjoy "business self help" books. Either they're brilliant and I'm annoyed I didn't write them or they're mediocre and I'm annoyed they're selling more than mine. They rarely speak to me as someone who runs a small business but spend most of my time with corporates. But this book was a joy to read. It really is relevant to anyone negotiating their way in the world today."

DAWN METCALFE, Managing Director, PDSi and author of *Managing the Matrix* and *The HardTalk™ Handbook*

"Navigating the myriad of career resources available to people in career transition can be daunting and overwhelming. With this book, Kristin provides a framework and an accompanying process that makes you feel like you are being guided and supported through your career journey. Having worked in the career development field for 20 years with very diverse clientele, I can honestly say that this book has something for everyone! This is a resource that I will use with clients, students, (my own teenage daughters) and anyone else that is contemplating a career move."

MARNIE GROENEVELD, Manager, Career Development Services, Manitoba Institute of Trades & Technology

"Best job search and career development book since I first read Dick Bolles' book, "What Color Is Your Parachute" in the 1970s which sold over 10 million copies. Today, Kristin's YouMap book is the most simple, thorough and practical guide. If you are unemployed, misemployed, or happily-employed working without purpose or meaning, get YouMap and find your way today."

BRIAN C. RAY, author of *Created for Good Works* and founder of Crossroads Career Network

"What a fantastic book! Kristin Sherry has done an excellent job putting together the content to help people discover themselves, then use their newfound power of potential to blaze their own path in this world.

I see how people at any stage of their career, from the newly-graduated college student to the mid-career professional, can use the plan from this book to determine how they can use their talents and skills to be everything that they want to be!"

PAUL CARNEY, entrepreneur, speaker and author of *Move Your Æ: Know, Grow, and Show Your Career Value*

"YouMap: Find Yourself. Blaze Your Path. Show the World! will quickly become your "go to" resource for personal growth and career development. Kristin Sherry simply and yet brilliantly "maps" out your strategy for a successful career and happy life. Run, do not walk, to get your hands on this book! As you transition throughout the different stages of your career and life, this book will be a gift that keeps on giving!"

DR. PATTY ANN TUBLIN, Amazon best-selling author and CEO & Founder, Relationship Toolbox LLC

"I have been hired by three companies, two of whom were multi-billion dollar companies, to complete turnarounds for failing communications departments. I credit in large part to my success in using assessments to identify each team member's strengths and passions. It wasn't about kicking people off the bus; it was about switching seats to place each individual in a position to provide their talents which in turn contributed to success. We went from the poorest performing to the highest performing departments in short order. When Kristin Sherry introduced YouMap, I immediately responded by telling her that every, and I mean every, company should invest in YouMaps for their associates. What a roadmap it provides to get the best out of everyone, and ensure they can be successful on behalf of those they serve."

GRETCHEN FIERLE, leadership author, *Fish Rot from the Head Down*

Contents

Dedication / Acknowledgments   8
Who This Book is For   10
Foreword   11
Introduction   17
Find Yourself   21
    Four Pillars of Career Satisfaction   22
    Discover Your Strengths   25
    Discover Your Values   52
    Discover Your Motivated Skills   59
    Discover How You're Wired   69
    The YouMap® Career Profile   89
    Create Your Own YouMap® Career Profile 91
    Case Study: Antonette, The Pharma Sales Rep   96
Blaze Your Path   107
    Introduction to O*NET   109
    Career Interest Profiler   109
    O*NET Occupational Database   113
    Job Boards and Job Descriptions   117
    Informational Interviews   119
    Volunteer Work   120
    The Side Hustle   121
    Stretch Projects   126
    Job Shadowing   127
    Mentoring   127
    Internships   128
    Work Attribute Preferences   129

Show the World!   137

Targeting Opportunities   138

Networking & Informational Interviews   141

The Personal Networking Sheet   144

Employer-Focused Cover Letters   150

Resumes Employers Want to See   154

Focusing Your Resume through Reflection by Patricia Edwards   156

Your Resume Tells a Story by Kerri Twigg   159

The Anatomy of an Amazing Resume by Kamara Toffolo   163

The Academic CV by Lisa Jones   176

All-Star LinkedIn Profiles   178

Crank Up Your Job Search with LinkedIn by Donna Serdula   182

Supplementary LinkedIn Sections by Lisa Jones   190

How to Wow Interviewers   195

Final Thoughts   214

About the Author   216

Want to Work with Kristin?   217

Tools & Resources   219

Dedication

For my children,

Tristan, my creative communicator and ideator,

Justin, my sensitive, yet brave and persistent competitor,

Kathryn, my independent and confident wonder,

Evelyn, my funny, curious and happy rainbow baby.

Watching you unfold into the unique people God intended you to be is the greatest gift.

Acknowledgments

All my thanks, first and foremost, to God for blessing me with the most amazing opportunities, such as writing this labor of love.

Thank you to my mom, dad, mother-and father-in-law, my extended family, friends, and colleagues who have always been so incredibly supportive of my book projects, and of me. I am so grateful to have a wonderful network of supportive people in my life!

I am grateful to Patricia Edwards, Kerri Twigg, Kamara Toffolo, Lisa Jones, and Donna Serdula for lending their deep expertise to this project. I appreciate each of you more than you know! What a tremendous amount of talent is packed into this group of people.

Thank you to my wonderful clients, Antonette and Anna, who gave me permission to tell a portion of their story in this book.

To my tremendous right hand, Stephanie Hall. If you didn't keep so many balls in the air with Virtus Career Consulting, this book would not exist. I couldn't have done this without you helping keep the business running!

Thank you, Beth Crosby, for lending your editing talents, yet again, to another one of my books. I appreciate your tremendous gift and how easy you are to work with.

My sincere appreciation to Jeff Haden for graciously taking time from his busy schedule to read this book and write the foreword.

Thank you to fellow author and friend, Justin Bariso, for introducing me to Jeff Haden, and for helping me grow as a person through his daily writing about emotional intelligence.

A huge thank you to my beta-readers Paul Carney, Roxanne Arriaza, Caroline Laird, Dawn Metcalfe, Jana Shields, and Marie Shadden who took time and care to give valuable feedback on the book.

I'd also like to thank my many connections and followers on LinkedIn who have been so supportive of my content contributions on the LinkedIn platform over the years. There are too many to list individually, but you and I know who you are!

A special thank you to my friend in sunny Cyprus, Pantelis Fouli, who helped me start on the road to good health this year.

I would be remiss if I did not thank author Ken Tasch, who offered to introduce me to his (and now my) publisher, Black Rose Writing.

Last, but never least, my best friend and incredibly supportive husband Xander for reading everything I write and being the greatest human being I've ever known.

Who This Book is For

This guide is for those trying to figure out what they do best, identifying who needs it most, and clearly conveying it to future employers, clients, or customers:

- **High school and college students** seeking clarity to choose a career path
- **Career changers** unsatisfied in their current career
- **Ambitious careerists** who need a competitive edge to get to the next step in their careers
- **Workforce re-entrants** such as stay-at-home moms and dads and caregivers to elder parents
- **Unemployed job seekers** who need help getting unstuck
- **Retirees** seeking direction for the final phase of their careers
- **Self-employed business owners** who need help discovering what they do best to differentiate themselves in a sea of competition

Foreword

When I saw Joe (not his real name, like the names that follow) my stomach lurched. The last time I'd seen him was twenty years ago.

The day I fired him.

Time is unkind to all but seemed especially unkind to Joe. His face was etched with lines and his eyes, once bright, were flat and lifeless. He shuffled over. I hesitantly reached to shake his hand.

"Hi Joe," I said. "How are you?"

He glanced away. "I guess I'm doing all right," he said.

Then he asked to borrow a twenty.

● ● ●

I was a manufacturing supervisor in the late 1990s when our department implemented an employee-empowerment program designed to shift as much responsibility as possible down to the team level. In time, employee committees became responsible for scheduling vacations, evaluating team members, and making hiring decisions. We became coaches and "facilitators" rather than supervisors.

I definitely supported the shift. I started on the shop floor, so I knew first-hand that employees at every level are always capable of handling greater responsibility than normally given. Plus, responsibility yields accountability, and accountability creates engagement: Empowerment fuels a powerful cycle that can take on an awesome life of its own.

And perhaps unsurprisingly, with a little training and guidance, some employees turned out to be far better leaders than many supervisors.

Still, at first most of our employees were skeptical. How much responsibility would we truly delegate? How much authority would we truly give up? At the first sign of trouble, would we stop guiding and start dictating?

In response, we went too far too fast, erring on the side of granting greater employee authority so they could learn to trust our commitment.

•••

Two weeks after Joe was hired, Mike, the evaluation coordinator for his team, came to my office to discuss Joe's performance.

"He's terrible," Mike said.

I asked for examples. We identified weaknesses and deficiencies. We brought Joe in to review his evaluation and list areas for improvement. It was standard stuff. Some employees are slower to catch on, others just need a reality check, but most come up to speed.

Two weeks later, Mike said Joe's performance had not improved. We put him on a performance plan, listing skills he needed to display and specific performance targets he needed to reach. Joe said he understood.

Later, though, Joe came to me and said, "I know I'm a little slow, but I also think they're too hard on me. It's not that I can't do the job. I think the real problem is they don't like me."

I found ways without being obvious to see better for myself, like hanging out on the line talking to operators while keeping one eye on Joe. (After all, I couldn't make it seem like I didn't trust the team's input.) He was definitely slow. Still, Mike's assessment seemed a little harsh.

Yet the team worked with him all day every day. No matter how hard I tried I would never know Joe's performance as well as they did. (Which, of course, was the reason we wanted employees to evaluate each other; the people who know your performance best are the people who work beside you.)

Two months into his 90-day probationary period Mike said Joe's performance was still sub-par. We brought Joe in, gave him a formal warning, and explained exactly what he needed to do in order to meet job requirements. We created a plan to provide additional training. He said he was trying hard but would try even harder.

A month later Mike turned in Joe's 90-day evaluation. "He doesn't cut it," he said. "We need to fire him."

"That's a big step," I said. "Are you sure?"

"I am," Mike said. "All of us are. Check out the individual reviews from the rest of the team."

According to their evaluations it was clear Joe hadn't met requirements. While I still had doubts, the proof was in front of me. The system had spoken. Joe needed to go.

I fired him.

He cried.

He said he had tried really hard. He said he knew he didn't fit in, but he couldn't help it. He told me he had never fit in, not in school, not with friends, not at jobs. He didn't know why but he always seemed to be the outsider. He felt his work wasn't the problem for other employees; working with him was the problem.

He begged for one more chance.

I told Joe we had given him a number of chances and unfortunately there were no chances left. I walked him to the plant entrance (we had to escort fired employees from the building, a "walk of shame" I always hated because it only served to further humiliate a person already devastated), shook his hand, and wished him well.

But I never forgot Joe. Unlike some other employees I fired, I sometimes questioned whether I had done the right thing. Sure, based on our system I had done everything "right," but had I actually done the right thing? Had I ignored the intuition that comes from long years of experience?

Had I let Joe become a victim of our drive towards empowerment?

●●●

What makes it worse is that some months earlier I facilitated a promotion committee meeting made up of employees using evaluation data to rank employees eligible for an open machine-operator position.

Gene emerged as the top candidate. Yet some in the room had doubts. "I know he looks good on paper," one explained, "but I don't think he has what it takes." Others agreed.

I didn't. "I understand you have concerns," I said, "but by every standard he's the best candidate. You can't bypass him based on feelings you can't quantify. How would you feel if that happened to you?" The dissenters grumbled but grudgingly agreed.

In the weeks to come, I had to step in a few more times. Several operators on his team felt he wasn't learning quickly enough and wanted him demoted. So I watched. Gene was slow, but once he knew how to do something, he *really* knew how. My experience in assessing employees -- experience shop floor employees didn't yet have -- told me all Gene needed was a little patience and a little time.

And I made sure he got it.

But I didn't do the same for Joe.

●●●

I reached for my wallet as Joe told me his story. He had worked a bunch of jobs but none that lasted. He had injured his knee but didn't have health insurance so it never healed properly. He talked about opportunities missed and turns not taken.

Later I thought about the role I had played in his life. Maybe if I had tried harder, or better trusted my judgment, things would have turned out differently. He may never have been an outstanding employee, but in time he might have turned out okay.

Working for what was at the time a leading employer in the area, holding a solid job with good benefits and plenty of overtime available... who knows what Joe's life might have been?

Would he have someday been like Gene, who turned out to be an outstanding operator and then went on to become a machinist with an incredible eye for detail and precision? Probably not. After all, Joe had under-performed in an unskilled position where effort was 90% of the success equation.

But who knows?

•••

Hiring, firing, disciplining, promoting... each is an everyday task for a leader. You need to make difficult and agonizing decisions about employees. You have to think, decide, act, and then put that decision behind you and move on.

That's the job.

Yet doing that job can dramatically change the life of other people. No matter how hard you try to get every decision that changes another person's life right, sometimes you won't. Those decisions -- and those regrets -- you soon realize you will live with forever.

Those decisions -- and those regrets -- you soon realize will also change *your* life. Hats off to all the people who try desperately to get every "people decision" right... and then pay the unseen price of wondering if they got one wrong.

Even though running a plant was a goal I chased for years and finally achieved, in time I realized that my career course – my YouMap – was no longer satisfying or fulfilling. Sure, it paid well. And the title on my business card was impressive.

But that job stopped working for me… and I finally found the courage to make a change.

Was it easy? Oh, hell no.

But it was worth it.

As it will be for you.

- Jeff Haden, author of *The Motivation Myth*, Inc. magazine contributing editor, LinkedIn Influencer and Ghostwriter.
Norfolk, Virginia, June 2018

YouMap®

Introduction

On Friday, February 15, 2018, I wrote the following post on the professional social media platform, LinkedIn.

Lena detested her job. And her manager was trying hard to get rid of her. She had a breakdown and was hospitalized for several days due to anxiety and stress.

Why didn't she quit? She felt like such an utter failure; her confidence was tanked. She couldn't think clearly about what she could do next. She couldn't present well in an interview in her state of fear and anxiety. She was also a single income household.

I spoke with Lena days after she left the psychiatric ward. I reviewed her StrengthsFinder results and shared what her top talents were and asked if she was able to use them in her job.

Nope. Never. Lena was in a terrible role misfit.

While discussing her true talents, Lena cried and said, "I have hope for the first time in months."

If you're struggling in your job, please know you have valuable strengths. Your talent is masked when you work against your natural gifting and operate from your weaknesses. You are NOT a failure in a poor job fit any more than you'd be a failure if your shoes didn't fit. You'd just get new shoes!

Don't believe the lies you tell yourself. Take time to figure out your unique brilliance. You were created for a purpose. Start with StrengthsFinder. Download and read your "Strengths Insight Guide." Discover who you really are.

When I clicked the Post button to submit this piece, I had no inkling it was about to go viral. A few days after submission, the post had well over one million views, 9,000 likes, and almost 1,000 comments. What was remarkable wasn't the statistics on the post; it was the stories and comments people shared.

Here are just a handful of examples:

- "Thank you for sharing this, reading the comments I realize that there are so many Lenas out there. I was Lena, once, too. The road to discovering your strengths and values is often very lonely and difficult, but oh what joy when you can finally shake off all that negativity and ignorance to uncover your true worth!! A blessing in disguise!" – Adriana
- "Such a great article. When your confidence and self-esteem are at rock bottom it can be almost impossible to focus on the positives. You can bounce back from an experience like this. Just keep believing in yourself and BELIEVE others when they say positive things about you. That's what will start to reshape you as your confidence builds. You may even find that the negative experience will make you stronger for the future. Good luck to all the 'Lenas' out there." – Lynne
- "Thank you for sharing this. Like others who commented here, I have been in similar situations primarily due to organization restructures. It's emotional enough to go through a re-org, but it's even harder when you're placed in a role where your skills are not a match. Figure out your unique brilliance—love this!" – Chris
- "Thank you, Kristin! This is a lot of help. As someone who has historically been in a misfit role and later laid off from a different role... It is so easy to convince yourself that you are not of value. We all have value. It is simply a matter of finding the right role." – Bethany

Do you love Mondays?

As a career consultant, I meet a lot of people who don't love Mondays. They are the motivation behind writing this book. Everywhere I go I hear some variation of Lena's story. I want to equip as many people as possible to avoid or escape misery in their careers because life is too short to dread Mondays!

YouMap®: Find Yourself. Blaze Your Path. Show the World! is the result of working with hundreds of people over the past six years to help them figure out what wasn't working in their careers. After listening to clients from across the globe and within many industries explain their dissatisfaction and work frustrations, I've identified four main pillars of career satisfaction.

These experiences led to the creation of the YouMap® career profile—a personalized plan to chart a better career course and make healthier and more satisfying career decisions based on your unique design.

This book seeks to accomplish three things:

Find Yourself – Uncover what do you do best and need most. It's all about your secret sauce. What makes you unique like no one else? You are gifted distinctly, and I want to help you know clearly, beyond a shadow of a doubt, the value you are positioned to bring.

Blaze Your Path – Identify feasible, desirable career options. Whether you work for yourself or someone else, what are feasible and desirable options that fit you best? How do you take your newly discovered self-awareness and give it legs? I'll show you how to discover a path you can confidently pursue to bring you the fulfillment you deserve.

Show the World! – Create your brand and clearly convey it to others. You can be the very best at what you do, but if you don't know how to tell your story, or you don't intentionally position yourself and your brand, others won't see it. This book will help you communicate your brilliance to others in a variety of ways: cover letters, your resume and LinkedIn profile, job interviews, exploratory conversations, networking, and on the job—to help you make the next move in your career with increased confidence and clarity.

Throughout the book, I will share case studies and stories of actual clients, a series of aha moments along their journeys of self-discovery, and how they leveraged these epiphanies to change their direction and take control of their lives.

The late American author and motivational speaker, Jim Rohn, said,

---

"If you don't design your own life plan, chances are you'll fall into someone else's plan. And guess what they have planned for you? Not much."

If you're tired of being a piece in someone else's puzzle, having other people make the decisions about what role you get plugged into, or what you should be working on, this book is for you.

If you feel you're drifting in your career, on autopilot with no one at the wheel, this book is for you.

If you're sick and tired of being sick and tired in your career, this book is for you.

If you feel completely lost in the woods without a map or compass, this book is for you.

If you decide to follow through to the end of this journey with me, be prepared to experience transformation, because that is the aim of this book—to help you transform your life. A big promise? You bet. And I'm prepared to deliver the inspiration, information, and application to help you make it happen.

Are you ready?

Find Yourself

"The unexamined life is not worth living." – Socrates, Greek Philosopher

From a young age, I had exposure to resources and tools that helped me figure out who I am and what I do best. I have been "DiSC'd" and "StrengthsFindered," "Myers-Brigged," and "Big Fived," just to name a few assessments. I became very aware of my personality, the way I tend to relate to people, my natural needs and motivations, and my strengths and challenges. Having a mother who was—and still is—a Master Board Certified Coach gave me a huge professional advantage. I gained not only insights but the language to explain these insights to others.

I believe both my awareness and ability to communicate who I was and what I did best was probably the number one contributing factor to pursuing roles I could excel in, as well as receiving offers in the thirteen jobs I interviewed for in my career. That awareness gave me great confidence going into interviews. I knew how to connect who I was and what I did best to what the role required. I also knew what roles to stay far away from.

I didn't realize until I hit my thirties how many people struggle to really know themselves, let alone articulate it clearly and confidently to other people. I would have been no different, quite frankly. The coaching I received from my mom was an extraordinary gift. Not only did I understand myself and what worked best for me, I had clarity on what I needed to avoid: the hallmarks of a poor career fit.

Last year, I met Anna—an intelligent, highly competent accounting professional and CPA. Anna contacted me because she was feeling completely stuck. She is a manager in an accounting department and had worked for her company for more years than she cared to admit. She was recently divorced and didn't have the energy to conduct a job search, but she was tired of dealing with all the "stuff" that accompanied her responsibilities.

Anna told me in our first phone call that she was overworked and her boss was about to give her even more responsibility. She also didn't like her schedule or working for her boss. She said they just didn't mesh in how they manage or do things. The problem, she told me, was that she wasn't sure what else she could do and couldn't easily and clearly put her finger on exactly what bothered her and what to avoid in the future.

Over the years I've used a variety of tools and assessments with clients. After working with hundreds of people, I've been able refine and hone the career discovery process and determine what works well. Every person I work with has different reasons why they are unfulfilled in his or her career. Yet, I have found that dissatisfaction always boils down to one or more of the four pillars of career satisfaction I explore with clients.

During that first call, I explained the four pillars of career satisfaction to Anna, and I will reveal them to you in this chapter.

Four Pillars of Career Satisfaction

Your Work Aligns with Your Strengths

 Your strengths are your natural, innate talents. Everyone is born with natural talents, but not everyone realizes the talents they have or actively works to develop them. Regardless, people perform better when something comes naturally to them, whether that's building rapport with new customers, figuring out solutions to problems, mentoring people to reach their potential, communicating thoughts and feelings effortlessly, or learning new skills and information quickly.

The Gallup Organization reports that people who use their strengths every day in their job are up to six times more engaged at work than employees who do not use their strengths daily. They define engaged employees as spending at least 4.5 hours of their day so absorbed in their work that time passes quickly for them.

Not only are people more engaged when they use their strengths, they're also up to three times more likely to say they have a good quality of life, according to Gallup polls. I will show you how to identify your top natural talents in the "Discover Your Strengths" section.

Your Work Aligns with Your Values

A chief source of career misery I have encountered with clients is misalignment between one's work and values. Simply put, your values dictate what's most important to you.

According to Gallup's 2017 State of the American Workplace report, "The modern workforce knows what's important to them and isn't going to settle. Employees are willing to look and keep looking for a company that's mission and culture reflect and reinforce their values."

Because each person is distinct, values vary widely. Therefore, it's important to reflect on what's most important to you. Listening to the advice of others can be helpful but be cautious of values-based advice. People who value security will steer you away from bold or adventurous risks. Others who value wealth and status might encourage you to pursue a career simply because of the salary potential.

Your work must align with your values, not the values of your spouse, best friend, sister, or parents. I will show you how to determine what's most important to you in the "Discover Your Values" section of this chapter.

Your Work Aligns with Your Motivating Skills

Skills are the abilities and expertise that contribute to your capacity to perform competently in a role, and those skills are portable across many jobs. In fact, according to Korn Ferry International, 85% of skills are transferable from job to job. In my experience, many career transition clients don't realize how many of their skills transfer to a role they haven't held in the past. Transferable skills are not tied to a job or function and can be used across a variety of settings and industries.

According to career development expert Richard Knowdell, our interest in performing certain skills on the job can be explained by four categories:

Motivated Skills – Skills you're good at and enjoy doing every day. For example, you might love conceptualizing, managing processes, writing, dealing with ambiguity, or working with numbers.

Burnout Skills – Skills you're good at but do not enjoy doing. For example, you might be proficient at working with numbers but find it tedious and draining.

Developmental Skills – Skills you would like to perform more but haven't had an opportunity to develop, such as managing others. Or perhaps you love managing your home budget but haven't had an opportunity with budget responsibility at work.

Low Priority Skills – These are the skills that no matter how much time you invest in them, you don't seem to significantly improve your skill level. That's OK, because you don't like to do them either!

I will show you how to clearly identify the skills you want to do more (and less) of in the "Discover Your Motivated Skills" section below.

Your Work Aligns with How You're Wired

 How you're wired refers to your natural preferences relative to interests, passion, and motivation. I often say "follow your passion" is misguided, though well-meaning, career advice because as you can see, passion is only one of the four pillars of career satisfaction. Therefore, the passion approach is too narrow to discover best career fit. I will help you reveal your interests and motivations in the "Discover How You're Wired" section.

Throughout this section, "Find Yourself," we'll dig deep into each of the four pillars of career satisfaction to equip you with substantial understanding and clarity on how to discover who you are and what makes you unique. Let's get started!

Discover Your Strengths

"Do not try to teach a pig to sing. It wastes your time and annoys the pig."
    – Robert Heinlein, Science Fiction Writer

The first pillar of career satisfaction is using your natural talents, or strengths, daily in your work.

Have you ever been in a job where you felt you were trying to fit a square peg into a round hole, and every day felt like an uphill climb? Or maybe you felt completely bored and unchallenged. When we're either struggling or stagnant, chances are good we're not using our natural strengths at work.

Suzanne wasn't.

When I met Suzanne, she explained she was miserable in her accounting job. Every day, and with every spreadsheet, she felt like she was dying a little bit more inside. Suzanne was an imaginative people person. She possessed deep empathy and was positive and encouraging. She was flexible and easy to get along with. She loved taking each day as it came and described the joy she felt in the fun and unexpected surprises life held when she allowed each day to unfold naturally. She loved to write poetry and fiction. Her accounting role, or the culture in which she was performing that role, didn't tap into these elements of Suzanne's strengths, personality, and interests.

When Suzanne was in high school, she submitted one of her stories to a writing contest sponsored by the local newspaper and won first place. Writing made her feel alive and enthusiastic. When she was graduated from high school, her parents thought her writing ambitions were childhood silliness and they told her they would pay for an education only in accounting or engineering. She picked what she considered the lesser of the two evils.

Suzanne's story is not uncommon. Many of us are lured from gifting the world with our natural abilities in exchange for pursuing "sensible" career paths by well-meaning loved ones—or even by ourselves—leaving our natural abilities largely untapped. I find this profoundly sad.

Let's get clear on what strengths are and are not. Your strengths are not the same as your skills. Skills are abilities you've learned, such as delegating, managing projects, giving presentations, supervising, multi-tasking, and negotiating.

Perhaps you're skilled at negotiating but the natural talent, or strength, underlying your negotiation skills could be quickly building rapport with people or using persuasive communication skills. Both building rapport and persuasive communication have multiple applications apart from the skill of negotiation. One or more strengths contribute to an ability to perform a skill well.

The Clifton StrengthsFinder

My preferred tool to help people discover their natural talents is the Clifton StrengthsFinder assessment created by the late Donald O. Clifton. StrengthsFinder was renamed the Clifton StrengthsFinder in his honor several years after his death. The American Psychological Association has also honored Donald Clifton with its presidential commendation as the "Father of Strengths-Based Psychology."

The Clifton StrengthsFinder was developed based on a forty year study by the Gallup Organization and is a language built around the thirty-four most common talents in humans. This assessment helps people discover and describe their natural talents, focusing on what's right with them.

Only one in thirty-three million people share the same top five strengths, and strengths are stable over a lifetime. That's not to say a person's top five strengths won't change. In fact, they often do. Everyone has more than five natural talents, and it's possible for strengths to move into the top five from the top ten if a person has been investing in a talent.

For example, if Strategic is within your top ten strengths but not in the top five, then you move into a new role that is more strategic in nature, it's possible for Strategic to move into your top five; while pushing another strength out of the top five.

If I could use only one assessment in my consulting practice, the Clifton StrengthsFinder would be it. Of all the assessments I've administered, and the thousands of client debriefs I've conducted, nothing elicits the reaction in people like this assessment.

I've had clients cry when I explain their strengths to them. Some react this way because they are emotionally overcome to learn the beauty and genius of talents they didn't have words to describe until that moment. Others, because a lightbulb went on, shedding light on a significant source of career misery. Still others experienced hope for the first time in ages by realizing they do, in fact, have value—despite how they've been made to feel at work, often by an unsupportive manager.

> A client named Lila wrote the following on LinkedIn after I debriefed her strengths:
>
> "Kristin Sherry made me fall in love tonight. With myself. With my potential. Because, apparently, I am AWESOME and rare. So are you, but I digress.
>
> I have these very specific strengths that play off of each other and allow me to really connect with people, bring them joy, help them to see what I see in them, and empower them with strategies to succeed. Kristin helped me identify the meaning of this set of strengths.
>
> In one Gallup Strengths coaching session, Kristin Sherry brought me so much self-awareness and affirmation, shed light on exactly why some parts of my career feel better than others, and what I should be doing next.
>
> I've now attached a .pdf of my personalized Gallup Strengths Report to my LinkedIn profile, which will allow future collaborators and clients to get to know why I am 1 in 33 million. That's a real number. And it's one in even more when you consider my personal context.
>
> Let me tell you something—nothing will make you feel more empowered than knowing exactly what you bring to the table in a way that no one else can."

Isn't it a wonderful gift that a person can learn to appreciate themselves like this? Let's go deeper so you can, too.

Strengths Themes

Each of the thirty-four strengths belongs in one of four theme categories. Not everyone has strengths in every category. Some people have strengths in two or three categories, for example. I've met a handful of people who have all five strengths in a single category.

The important thing to realize is there is no good or bad organization of your strengths. Instead, understanding where your strengths are themed reveals important insights about you.

The four strength categories are:

| Relating Themes | Influencing Themes | Executing Themes | Thinking Themes |

This chart shows each of the thirty-four strengths by theme category.

Relating	Influencing	Executing	Thinking
Explain how people **build connections** with others	Explain how an individual **moves others to action**	Explain what pushes an individual toward results	Explain how a **person analyzes** the world
Adaptability	Activator	Achiever	Analytical
Connectedness	Command	Arranger	Context
Developer	Communication	Belief	Futuristic
Empathy	Competition	Consistency	Ideation
Harmony	Maximizer	Deliberative	Input
Inclusiveness	Significance	Discipline	Intellection
Individualization	Self-Assurance	Focus	Learner
Positivity	WOO	Responsibility	Strategic
Relator		Restorative	
PEOPLE-FACING STRENGTHS		**INWARD-FACING (TASK) STRENGTHS**	

Following are detailed descriptions for each of the thirty-four strengths, by category. If you haven't yet taken the Clifton StrengthsFinder assessment, try to identify which strengths you think might show up in your Top 5 based on the descriptions. If you have taken it, read the descriptions and see if you agree with how they describe you.

Relating Themes

Explain how people build connections with others

The Relating strengths explain how you build connections with others. Everyone who has one of these nine strengths enjoys building connections with people. However, those connections are created differently based on which strength the person is using. People with Relating themes prefer to work collaboratively with others, rather than independently. I have no relating themes, yet I connect with people. Not having relating themes does not mean you're incapable of relating with people.

The following nine strengths are categorized as Relating themes:

Adaptability – You take things as they come. You can respond willingly to the demands of the moment; you don't resent sudden requests or unforeseen detours. You stay productive when the demands pull you in many directions at once. You need variety in your work.

Descriptors: flexible, comfortable in times of change, easy to get along with, goes with the flow

Connectedness – You have faith in the links between all things. You believe there are few coincidences and almost every event has a reason. You are a bridge builder among people who share differences.

Descriptors: spiritual, "doesn't sweat the small stuff," strong faith, always looks at the big picture, helps others see purpose

Developer – You recognize and cultivate the potential in others. You see each small improvement. Your goal is to help others experience success. You look for ways to challenge others and devise interesting experiences that can stretch them and help them grow.

Descriptors: grows talent in others, teacher, coach, enjoys helping others succeed, invests in others

Empathy – You can sense the emotions of others, feel what they are feeling, see the world through their eyes. You hear unvoiced questions and anticipate their needs. For this reason, others are drawn to you.

Descriptors: creates trust, brings healing, knows just what to say/do, customizes approaches to others

Harmony – You look for consensus. Rather than conflict, you want agreement. You look for common ground, believing that imposing views on others wastes time. You steer clear of debate, preferring to talk about practical, down-to-earth matters on which everyone can agree.

Descriptors: negotiator, can see both sides of a situation, excellent at asking questions, able to arrive at consensus, great facilitator

Includer – You accept others, are aware when they feel left out, and make an effort to include them. You like to include as many people as possible. You cast few judgments, believing we are all important and fundamentally the same.

Descriptors: invites others in, caring, engages others, sensitive, takes up for others

Individualization – You are intrigued with the unique qualities of each person and have a gift for figuring out how people can work together productively. You focus on differences among people, seeing their strengths and drawing out the best in each person.

Descriptors: sees the uniqueness in all individuals, intuitively knows one size doesn't fit all, appreciates the differences in others

Positivity – Your enthusiasm is contagious. You are upbeat and create excitement; people want to be around you because you lighten their spirits. You find ways to make everything more vital and inject drama into every project. You don't always feel positive inside (You're human!), but you desire to express positivity toward others. It's important for people with this strength to avoid negative environments as it will feel toxic.

Descriptors: enthusiastic, lighthearted, energetic, generous with praise, optimistic

Relator – You enjoy close friendships with others, finding deep satisfaction working hard with friends to achieve a goal. For you, a relationship has value only if it is genuine. You want to understand others' feelings, their goals, their fears and their dreams.

Descriptors: caring, trusting, a great friend, forgiving, generous

Influencing Themes

Explain how an individual moves others to action

The Influencing strengths explain how you motivate or influence others to action. Again, not everyone will have strengths in this category. However, everyone who has one of these eight strengths can persuade or influence people in some way; their mode of persuasion and influence varies based on the specific influencing strength. People with Influencing themes are adept at accomplishing their goals through people.

It's also important to be aware that people who do not have Influencing strengths in their Top 5 tend to dislike the responsibility of influencing and persuading people at work. I'll talk more about this later.

Activator – You make things happen by turning thoughts into actions. Each day—365 days of the year—you must accomplish something meaningful. You believe that action is the best device for learning. You know you will be judged by what you get done—and it pleases you.

Descriptors: self-starter, fire starter, energy source, fearless

Command – You have presence. You can take control of a situation and make decisions. Once your goal is set, you feel restless until you have aligned others with you. Confrontation does not frighten you because you know it's the first step to resolution.

Descriptors: charismatic, direct, driven, inspirational, easy to follow, clear, concise

Communication – You like to explain, describe, host, write, and speak in public. You generally find it easy to put thoughts into words. You are a good conversationalist and presenter. People like to listen to you. Your words pique their interest and inspire them to act.

Descriptors: storyteller, great presence, easy to talk to, energizer, entertaining, charismatic

Competition – You measure your progress against the performance of others. You strive to win and revel in contests. You like other competitors because they invigorate you. Although you are gracious to your fellow competitors, you compete to win. For you, losing is not an option.

Descriptors: driven, motivated, number one, measurement oriented, winner

Maximizer – You seek to transform something strong into something superb. Excellence, not average, is your measure. You don't want to take something from below average to slightly above average when that same effort could make something good, great.

Descriptors: mastery, success, excellence, enjoys working with the best

Self-Assurance – You are confident in your abilities; your inner compass tells you you're right. You know that your perspective is unique and distinct. No matter what the situation, you know the right decision. This theme lends you an aura of certainty.

Descriptors: self-confident, strong inner compass, risk taker

Significance – You want to be important in the eyes of others; you want to be recognized and heard, to stand out, to be known. You want to associate with others who are credible, professional, and you will push them to achieve until they are.

Descriptors: seeks outstanding performance, does things of importance, independent

WOO (Winning Others Over) – You love the challenge of meeting new people. You enjoy breaking the ice and making a connection with another person. In your world there are no strangers, just friends you haven't met yet.

Descriptors: outgoing, people oriented, networker, rapport builder

Executing Themes

Explain what pushes an individual toward results

Executing strengths explain what drives an individual toward results. However, the motivation behind results varies depending on which of these nine strengths an individual possesses. People with Executing strengths are Doers. If you don't have any Executing strengths and find yourself in the role of an executer or implementer, that's probably not very satisfying to you.

Achiever – You have a great deal of stamina and work hard. You take tremendous satisfaction from being busy and productive. Your drive is the power supply that causes you to set the pace and define productivity levels for others.

Descriptors: tireless, strong work ethic, leads by example, go-getter, hungry

Arranger – You can organize but also have flexibility that complements it. You like to figure out how all the pieces and resources can be arranged for maximum productivity. You try to figure out the best way to get things done. You can manage things as they move or change—you can manage chaos.

Descriptors: flexible, organizer, juggler, aligns and realigns tasks to find the most productive configuration possible, efficient, conductor

Belief – You have core values that are unchanging. Out of these values emerge a defined purpose for your life. Your friends call you dependable and easy to trust. Your work must mesh with your values.

Descriptors: passionate, steadfast, knows where he or she stands, altruistic, family oriented, ethical, responsible

Consistency (formerly called Fairness) – You are keenly aware of the need to treat people the same by setting up clear rules and adhering to them. In contrast to the world of special favors, you believe people function best in a consistent environment where everyone knows what is expected.

Descriptors: just, problem-solver, policy maker

Deliberative – You are best described by the serious care you take in making decisions or choices. You identify dangers, weigh their relative impact, and then plan accordingly. You minimize risk.

Descriptors: anticipates obstacles, makes solid decisions, plans for the unexpected

Discipline – You enjoy routine and structure, focusing on timelines and deadlines. You break long-term projects into a series of specific short-term plans, and you work through each plan diligently. You create order as a way to continue progress.

Descriptors: highly productive and accurate because of ability to structure, breaks down complex into steps, great planner, promotes efficiency

Focus – You take a direction, follow through and make the corrections necessary to stay on track. You prioritize, then act. You regularly set goals that become your compass; focus forces you to be efficient. When others wander, you bring them back to the goal.

Descriptors: point person, disciplined, purposeful, laser-like precision, identifies important areas quickly, goal setter and goal getter

Responsibility – You take psychological ownership of what you say you will do, feeling duty bound to follow it through to completion. This near obsession for doing things right and your impeccable ethics create your reputation as utterly dependable. In short, you do the right thing, do things right, and do what you say you're going to do.

Descriptors: committed, accountable, independent, trusted, conscientious

Restorative – You are adept at dealing with problems. You enjoy the challenge of analyzing symptoms, identifying what's wrong, and finding the solution. It energizes you. You enjoy revitalizing things, people, or processes.

Descriptors: problem solver, troubleshooter, finds improvements and solutions

Thinking Themes

Explain how a person analyzes the world

The Thinking strengths explain how you analyze the world. Those who possess one or more of the eight Thinking themes are exactly that—Thinkers. They need to be in roles that don't merely execute but have some mental activity behind it. Early careerists with a lot of Thinking themes are often frustrated by the "pay your dues" mentality in many corporations, relegating them to worker bee roles when they'd rather be doing the mental heavily lifting.

Analytical – You search for reasons and causes. You think about all the factors that could affect a situation. Others see you as logical and rigorous. You do not want to destroy others' ideas, but you do insist that their theories be sound.

Descriptors: thinks things through, smart, deep, thorough, comfortable with numbers, figures, and charts

Context – The past is important to you because it helps you understand the present. By thinking back, you see the blueprints for the present, and realize what the original intent was. You must discipline yourself to ask the questions and allow the blueprints to emerge.

Descriptors: has robust historical frame of reference, learns lessons from the past, knows how things came to be, can leverage knowledge of the past

Futuristic – You are inspired by what could be and inspire others with your vision. You see in detail what the future might hold, and it pulls you forward. You make the picture as vivid as possible for others to see and keep asking, "Wouldn't it be great if…?"

Descriptors: imaginative, creative, visionary, inspiring

Ideation – You are fascinated by ideas and find connections between seemingly disparate phenomena. Others may label you creative, original or conceptual, or even smart. What you are sure of is that ideas are thrilling.

Descriptors: improves on the existing, learns quickly, agile mind

Input – You have a craving to know more and often collect and archive information. You keep acquiring, compiling and filing stuff away because it's interesting and keeps your mind fresh, without knowing when and why you might need it.

Descriptors: great resource, knowledgeable, excellent memory, mind for detail, collects interesting things, excellent conversationalist

Intellection – You like to think; you like mental activity. You enjoy time alone because you can reflect. This introspection lets you compare what you are doing with all the thoughts and ideas that your mind conceives. This mental hum is a constant in your life.

Descriptors: excellent thinker, enjoys musing, capable of deep and philosophical thought, able to work alone

Learner – You have a great desire to continuously improve. Learning enables you to thrive in dynamic work environments where you are asked to take on short project assignments and learn a lot about the new subject matter in a short period of time.

Descriptors: always learning, catches on quickly, interested in many things, finds life intriguing

Strategic – You find alternative ways to proceed, sorting through clutter to find the best route. This ability cannot be taught. You play out alternative scenarios allowing you to see around the next corner. You discard paths that lead nowhere.

Descriptors: good judgment, identifies risk, sees the shortest path to a goal, quickly identifies patterns

Now that I've introduced the strengths by category, I'd like to address some commonly asked questions before we go further into strengths exploration.

Common Strengths Q & A

Where can I purchase the Clifton StrengthsFinder assessment?

tinyurl.com/yar7d7f4

I've taken StrengthsFinder in the past. Do I need to retake it?

I suggest retaking the assessment if you've had a significant life or job change or if you took the assessment more than three years ago.

I've taken the Clifton StrengthsFinder assessment before. I'm trying to take it again and I'm getting an error message.

Gallup allows one Top 5 assessment completion per account created on their website. They prefer you purchase the "All 34 CliftonStrengths" report (which is more expensive) if you've already taken the Top 5. To retake the Top 5 assessment you'll need to create a new account using a different email address.

I'm considering changing jobs. How can I tell if I have the right strengths?

Remember, your strengths are only one aspect of the four pillars of career fit. In addition, multiple combinations of strengths could prove successful in a role. An example is project management. If a person has Discipline (Executing theme), Achiever (Executing theme), Learner (Thinking theme), Consistency (Executing theme), and Input (Thinking theme), they have three Executing and two Thinking strengths. This person will approach project management as a Doer and a Thinker.

Perhaps the greatest contribution they bring is the ability to keep projects moving forward and planning out complex projects into work breakdown structures based on their Discipline talent. Another contribution stems from the Input strength because people with Input are great at taking in information and have a mind for details and facts.

However, a person with Influencing and Relating strengths could be just as effective in a project manager role, approaching his or her job in a completely different way. The people-facing talents would create a tendency to concentrate more on the project team than tasks. Let's say a person's strengths are Relator,

Activator, Individualization, Arranger, and Positivity.

The approach to project management in this case would be flexibility and an ability to calmly handle chaos (Arranger), while influencing people's sense of urgency to initiate their tasks through the Activator talent. The Relator strength would equip them to find common ground and build connections easily across the organization. People-facing and inward-facing strengths can both contribute to success in the same role.

Where strengths become more exclusive is in specialist or expert roles. Specialists tend to perform a narrower set of tasks than generalists do. Individual expert roles such as IT, compliance, engineering, quality assurance, and architectural design often have a dominant set of strengths correlated with their roles. For example, engineering is an expert occupation and requires at least one of a few strengths such as Analytical (fact-finding), Deliberative (risk mitigating), Restorative (problem-solving).

Do I need to purchase "All 34 CliftonStrengths," or should I purchase only the Top 5?

The Top 5 report is usually sufficient for anyone who wants to understand or explain his or her own strengths. Strengths are useful for job interviews, personal development, building teams, and many other applications. One situation when it might be necessary to view the full thirty-four strengths is when you are hiring or if you're considering a role where you know a strength is of paramount importance.

For example, I'm often asked what strengths are required to have a job like mine. As a career consultant I help career changers who are often uncertain of their future. As a Leadership Consultant I help leaders solve complex challenges.

While coaches can be successful with a wide variety of different strength profiles, helping people figure out work they're wired for, determining how to get from where they are now to where they want to be, and helping leaders solve intractable challenges requires strategic thinking.

If you're interested in a consulting career and Strategic is not in your Top 5, you can purchase the "All 34 CliftonStrengths" report to see if it appears in the Top 10.

I don't agree with my results. What should I do?

I've had two people disagree with some, but not all, of their strengths in approximately two thousand strength discussions. The questions I ask are, "Were you distracted when you took the assessment?" and "Did you let quite a few questions pass without answering?" The assessment is timed and provides you with twenty seconds to respond to each statement. "Did you answer the questions as you thought you should, rather than how you really are?"

If the answer is no to the above questions, have someone who knows you well read your "Strengths Insight Guide" report, downloadable from your dashboard at www.gallupstrengthscenter.com, and provide his or her opinion on how well each strength represents you.

If the person who reads your report agrees your report doesn't sound like you, retake it. Again, I've never had one person completely disagree with all five strengths, and only one person out of two thousand chose to retake it. They agreed with their next set of results, so it's also possible that person misread the instructions or the assessment statements.

Is there rhyme or reason to the order of my strengths? Is the first one listed my strongest?

This question will be fully answered in the next section, "Identifying Your Driver, Passenger, and Fuel Strengths."

My strengths sound just like me, but how do I explain this to other people, such as interviewers?

The "How to Wow Interviewers" section of "Show the World!" discusses this and provides the link to an instructional video.

Identifying Your Driver, Passenger, and Fuel Strengths

After you've taken the StrengthsFinder assessment, you'll have access to download a free report from the Gallup website called the "Strengths Insight

Guide." This report can be found at www.gallupstrengthscenter.com on the main page after logging in, under Reports and Tools, shown here:

We'll use this report to complete an exercise to order your strengths by intensity (most-to-least strong). About 50% of the time, after clients read their report, they will order the list of strengths differently than the default rank order provided by Gallup. While you're on the Gallup website, also download the "Strengths Insight and Action Planning Guide." It has reflection questions you should find helpful.

I was meeting with a friend for brunch recently, and she brought her strengths results to discuss with me. Tammy's report had Includer listed first as her top strength, but after reading her report she felt Strategic was the most compelling of the five.

What's the difference? Well, your number one strength is going to be the one that's most important for you to use every day. It sets your priorities. In Tammy's example, Strategic, which is the ability to generate alternatives and figure out the best available option, compels her more than the ability to draw in people who feel left out (Includer).

Includer is one of her strengths. She just identifies more with Strategic. This makes Strategic the strongest of Tammy's top five strengths.

The order of your strengths is important. Your top (strongest) strength is like the Driver of a car. The Driver is in control. He decides the route to take and how fast to drive. He determines whether to make a stop on the way to the destination and perhaps even controls the radio.

The Driver calls the shots.

Just as the Driver of a car decides where the car is heading, your Driver strength sets your priorities every day in your work because it has greater intensity than the other strengths.

Continuing the car analogy, your strengths can be organized as follows:

• Driver: This is the strength that you would consider very strong.
• Passengers: These are the next two strengths you would consider strong. However, they aren't as strong as your number one strength.
• Fuel: These two strengths are moderate in intensity.

Now, picture the Driver behind the wheel of the car. The passengers sit in the back seat like co-pilots and help the driver navigate the car. They aren't in control, but they can influence the Driver.

For example, when I pick up my son, Justin, from school, my daughter, Kathryn, and I always pass a Bruster's Ice Cream store. She almost always asks if we can stop for ice cream before or after we pick up Justin. And I almost always say no. However, in the past couple of years I've stopped twice in response to her plea for ice cream. As a Passenger she can influence me, the Driver. The Passenger is not as intense as the Driver but still has influence.

Fuel strengths are the most moderate in strength of your top five. In fact, the Fuel in a car doesn't have any interest in trying to influence the Driver where it should go. It provides the gas needed to reach the destination and nothing more. The Fuel strengths give you the push you need to accomplish your priorities, but these strengths work in service to the Driver.

Let me explain with an example. If Achiever is my Driver strength, my priority every single day is to be tremendously productive. If Achiever is a Fuel, I am busy and productive each day but with much less intensity. My number one priority is not to be productive. The ambition I have serves the greater strength (Driver) to accomplish its goals. If my Driver were WOO (Winning Others Over), my priority would be to meet and interact with everyone whose path I crossed that day. Achiever as a Fuel would give me the stamina to network and schmooze with people throughout the day.

I'll explain more about your Driver, Passenger, and Fuel strengths, but first let's do a ranking exercise to see how you would order your strengths.

 After taking the Clifton StrengthsFinder assessment, open your "Strengths Insight Guide" and read each paragraph under "What makes you stand out?" Underline or highlight each phrase or sentence that describes you—you probably won't agree strongly with all statements.

The image below illustrates a strength in my own "Strengths Insight Guide"—Ideation—along with its description. One of the things that makes this report valuable is the description is customized to you. Another person with the Ideation strength will have variations in the description in his or her report because elements of some of your other top strengths are woven into the description, which is why this report resonates so strongly with the person who took the assessment.

Ideation

SHARED THEME DESCRIPTION

People who are especially talented in the Ideation theme are fascinated by ideas. They are able to find connections between seemingly disparate phenomena.

YOUR PERSONALIZED STRENGTHS INSIGHTS
What makes you stand out?

Instinctively, you typically generate inventive ideas for new projects, especially those that require upgrading things. When you are challenged to be an innovative thinker, you feel valued. Chances are good that you engage life with gusto. Bursting with creativity, you approach assignments, tasks, projects, opportunities, or problems. You like to take the innovative path rather than follow the traditional and tried-and-true ways of doing things. It's very likely that you sometimes are aware of the views specific people have of you. This partially explains why you keep expanding your vocabulary to include elaborate terminology and complicated words. You might argue that your use of language causes certain individuals to think well of you. Because of your strengths, you contribute many innovative ideas to the group during brainstorming sessions. You tend to be highly imaginative when proposals are fully heard and any criticism is reserved for a later time. By nature, you might pay particular attention to what certain people think of you. Perhaps you intentionally use complicated words or specialized terminology to position yourself as an expert or a professional in the minds of others. Sometimes you use language to your advantage when you hope to influence, confront, make demands of, or issue orders to specific individuals. Maybe your vocabulary allows you to speak with a bit more authority than usual.

After you complete the underlining exercise for your first strength:

Reflect: Is this strength very strong, strong, or moderately strong in you? Note your impression on your report next to the strength, such as VS for very strong, S for strong, and MS for moderately strong.

 Repeat the underlining exercise for the next strength listed in your "Strengths Insight Guide."

Reflect: Is this a little stronger, equally strong, or a little less strong than the first strength? Again, note your answer by marking very strong (VS), strong (S), or moderate (M) next to the strength.

Repeat the underlining and comparison exercise for all five strengths, determining if they are slightly stronger, equal to, or slightly less strong than the others. This will help you order the strengths. Some people agree with the ranking Gallup provided, while others reorder them. Try not to worry about getting the order wrong. It's not black and white, and you can always reorder your strengths if the guide doesn't feel accurate.

Take a moment, now, to download the Coachee Strengths Worksheet at MyYouMap.com.

Next, enter your strongest theme into the Driver section on page two of the Coachee Strengths Worksheet you downloaded, shown here:

Read about each of your strengths. Which of these feels strongest to you? This Strength is your **Driver**.

My **Driver** is _____.

Here's **how I use my driver** every day to achieve my priorities:

Note: Sometimes people have two Drivers. This occurs when you simply cannot choose one strength as the most dominant and consider two strengths as equally very strong. In this case, the two strengths work like a student driver education car, where the student and the instructor can take over control of the car. One strength sets your priorities in some situations, and the other strength takes over in other situations.

No right or wrong order exists, but it would be highly unusual to have three Drivers. Choose one, ideally, and two if they are tied for top spot.

Place the next strongest themes in the Passenger section of the strengths worksheet, and the moderately strong themes in the Fuel section, shown here:

My next two strongest Strengths are _____ and _____ .

These are my **Passengers**. Here is how they work together with my **Driver** to help me achieve my priorities:

My last two Strengths are _____ and _____ .

These are my **Fuel**, and this is how they reinforce and support my **Driver/Passenger combinations**:

Tip: If you're struggling to determine your Driver (very strong), Passengers (strong) and Fuel (moderate) strengths, look at your "Strengths Insight Guide" to see which strengths have the most or least amount of underlining.

Keep in mind you don't use your strengths one at a time. Your Driver and Passenger strengths combine, or work together, like cogs work together to make the hands of an analog watch move.

Put another way, when you combine primary colors such as yellow and blue, you create green. Similarly, your strengths combine to create new strength behaviors. I call these Strength Personas.

Your Strengths Personas (sometimes referred to as Strength Blends) are what people will notice about you as your predominant talents. Let me explain how to identify them.

Discovering Your Strength Personas

Let's review an example to illustrate how to discover your Strength Personas using the following strengths. WOO is very strong, so it's the Driver. Ideation and Strategic are strong, so they are the Passengers. Communication and Responsibility are moderately strong, so they are the Fuel strengths.

Driver – WOO (Winning Others Over)
Passenger 1 – Ideation
Passenger 2 – Strategic
Fuel 1 – Communication
Fuel 2 – Responsibility

In this example, the person's Driver, or strongest priority, is WOO—to influence people and win them over.

Imagine the Passengers, Ideation and Strategic, are sitting in the back seat of the car. We'll combine each passenger, one at a time, with the Driver. When Ideation steps out of the backseat of the car and sits up front with WOO, we combine the tendency to win people over (WOO) with the tendency to generate inventive ideas (Ideation). In other words, WOO + Ideation is the strength of winning people over to your ideas.

This is just one behavioral possibility of WOO + Ideation. Another possibility could be generating ideas for innovative networking approaches, such as observing and mirroring other people's body language.

Now, let's send Ideation to the back seat and have Strategic sit in the front seat with WOO in our example. This strength combination of WOO and Strategic might be creating key partnerships to help a person achieve their goals, for example, strategic networking or figuring out the best way (Strategic) to attract new partnerships (WOO).

In our example, the Fuel, Communication and Responsibility, help the Driver (WOO) achieve its goals through effective verbal skills (Communication) and quality-oriented, ethical, and accountable behavior (Responsibility) when trying to influence others, as well as doing what they say they are going to do when they partner with other people.

Now, after seeing an example, combine your first Driver and Passenger strength pairing and consider how these strengths work together to form your strength personas, or strength blends. Imagine yourself at work, school, or in personal life situations as if you're watching yourself in a movie. Observe how you tend to think, respond, or behave. Reference the descriptions in your "Strengths Insight Guide" to help you conjure up examples of your strengths in action.

Next, think about what it's like when your other Driver and Passenger strength combination work together. How are you thinking, responding, and behaving with this other strength blend?

Let me provide another example of Strengths Blends. Stephanie is my client services manager and is also certified in student coaching. Here are her strengths:

Drivers: Empathy and Belief
Passengers: Includer and Positivity
Fuel: Developer

Stephanie has four strength personas when you combine her two passengers with her two drivers, as follows:

Empathy (Driver) + Includer (Passenger)
Empathy (Driver) + Positivity (Passenger)
Belief (Driver) + Includer (Passenger)
Belief (Driver) + Positivity (Passenger)

I asked Stephanie to consider how she behaves, to put herself in the scene, when each Passenger influences each of her Drivers. Let's review the combination above in bold as an example.

When **Empathy** and **Positivity** work together, she puts herself in the other person's shoes and feels what it's like to be in their situation (Empathy) and then she attempts to encourage that person to lift their spirits (Positivity).

Stephanie's Fuel strength is Developer: the natural teacher, mentor, trainer, and coach. She uses Developer as a supporting strength to mentor people as she attempts to lift their spirits.

Reflect: How do your Fuel strengths help each of your Driver/Passenger strength combinations?

My Strengths Insights

You live with your strengths every day. The answers are already inside of you, so trust yourself!

Capture your insights:

_____

_____

_____

_____

_____

_____

_____

_____

_____

_____

_____

_____

_____

_____

_____

_____

_____

_____

I will go into greater detail in section two, "Blaze Your Path," about the practical application of using your strengths information to identify best fitting roles. Section three, "Show the World!" will teach you how to tell your strengths story to others.

Discover Your Values

"And every day, the world will drag you by the hand, yelling, 'This is important! And this is important! And this is important! You need to worry about this! And this! And this!' And each day, it's up to you to yank your hand back, put it on your heart and say, 'No. This is what's important.'" – Iain Thomas, Author

---

The second pillar of career satisfaction is your work aligns with what you value most.

I met Ryan in 2017 and discovered his top value was honesty. He defined honesty as honoring what you say you're going to do and owning your mistakes. Honesty was so important to Ryan that he chose to step away from a profitable career because he had been dealing with a dishonest customer. He couldn't be in an environment where he had to interact with someone who was dishonest with him.

Therefore, he called it quits and stepped into unfamiliar territory: unemployment. (I'm happy to report he did not remain unemployed long!)

A job that uses your strengths and has all the skills you enjoy will still be a poor fit if the role, your manager, or the workplace culture violates your values. Take a moment, now, to complete the following values exercise to discover what's most important to you. Your values are the most direct way to answer the question, "Who am I?"

Identify and Prioritize Your Values

As you complete this values exercise, think of examples from both your work and personal lives. This will provide a holistic approach to your answers. You can also download this exercise at MyYouMap.com.

Step 1: Identify times when you were happiest or fulfilled

- What were you doing?
- Were you with other people? Who?
- What other factors contributed to your happiness, pride, and fulfillment?
- What is it you value about what you listed? In other words, what does it provide you?

Tip: If what you've listed is a thing or an activity, drill deeper by asking yourself, "What does that thing or activity give me?" A person, place, or thing is not a value; it's a means to an end to achieve the value. For example, family is a thing, not a value. What does your family provide that you value? Love? Connection? Belonging?

Step 2: Determine 5-10 values based on your experiences of happiness and fulfillment

Use the following list of common personal values to get you started—aim for no more than ten values. You might find some values naturally combine, such as service and community, or honesty and trust. Group similar values together, if desired. Also, there's no need to limit yourself to this list.

Authenticity	Competency	Honesty	Openness	Self-Respect
Achievement	Contribution	Humor	Optimism	Service
Adventure	Creativity	Influence	Peace	Spirituality
Authority	Curiosity	Inner Harmony	Pleasure	Stability
Autonomy	Determination	Justice	Poise	Success
Balance	Fairness	Kindness	Popularity	Status
Beauty	Faith	Knowledge	Recognition	Trust
Boldness	Fame	Leadership	Religion	Wealth
Compassion	Friendships	Learning	Reputation	Wisdom
Challenge	Fun	Love	Respect	
Citizenship	Growth	Loyalty	Responsibility	
Community	Happiness	Meaningful Work	Security	

Step 3: Prioritize your values

This step is probably the most difficult. It's also the most important because when you're faced with a decision you can't always satisfy your entire list of values. Therefore, knowing which values are the most important is helpful.

 First, make a list of your top values, in any order.

Next, look at the first two values in your list and reflect, "If I could satisfy only one of these, which would I choose?" For example, if I could have all the Achievement I wanted, but no Freedom, or all the Freedom I wanted, but no Achievement, which would I choose? Do this with your list of values of course, not my examples!

Try to visualize an actual situation. For example, if you compare the values of Service and Stability, imagine you were trying to decide if you should sell your house and move to another country to do highly valued foreign aid work or keep your house and volunteer to do charity work close to home. If you value stability over service, you might choose the latter and not wish to create instability by selling your home. Alternatively, you might choose the former option and travel abroad if you value service over stability.

Keep working through the list, comparing each value against the next, until your list is in the priority order that makes sense for you.

To complete the values reflection, start with the first value in your prioritized list and reflect on these questions:

What does [value] mean to me?

It's important to clearly define and record what this value represents to you.

Do I desire this value to be reciprocated in the workplace by my manager and/or team members?

Reciprocal values are important because for the value to be honored, you not only need to experience the value in the workplace personally, but it should be returned to you. For example, honesty is always a reciprocal value. You value being honest, and you expect others to be honest in return.

Other examples of values that tend to be reciprocal include hard work, teamwork, dependability, and loyalty. Example values that might not be reciprocal, but are important to the individual, could be patriotism, health and fitness, and making a difference. One person who values patriotism might not require others to feel the same, whereas another person, such as a member of the military, might expect this reciprocity.

Reciprocity is a personal determination—with no right or wrong answer. If a value is reciprocal, place an asterisk next to it.

Was/Is this value honored or violated in my role, by my manager, and in the workplace culture?

If you're self-employed, you might want to apply this value to your client or customer.

I use the word honored to convey the value is respected. I use the word violated to convey the value is dishonored or disrespected.

Looking across these three levels—role, manager, and company—is crucial when evaluating values alignment for your workplace situation.

Why?

If your values don't align with your role, **a career transition** might be needed. For example, if you're responsible for customer payment collections and you value empathy, that's going to be tough turf for you.

If your values don't align with your manager's values, that situation will likely require **a team or manager change**, perhaps within the same company, or even outside the company. For example, if honesty is in your top values and your manager isn't transparent or open, that is not going to be something you can easily overlook.

If your values don't mesh well with the workplace culture, even a good manager won't be able to shield you from the fallout indefinitely. An organizational-level values misalignment most often requires **departing the organization.**

Asking these three questions pinpoints which values are misaligned, not reciprocated (if reciprocal), and at what level (role/manager/organization) the disconnect occurs. This exercise provides crucial information to reveal a key source of dissatisfaction.

Once you identify the values being violated, and at what level, the most obvious consideration is if you need to depart your role, your manager, or your organization. I highly recommend addressing the situation if it's at the manager level by giving feedback. You shouldn't assume your manager won't be responsive until you try. A conversation is much less work than a job search! *The HardTalk™ Handbook*, by Dawn Metcalfe, is a must-read guide to having difficult conversations more effectively.

If values are not aligned at the role level, you might discuss with your manager if changes could be made to your role. This option won't be viable for everyone, but my mother always taught me if you don't ask, you don't get!

Once you have a clear idea of your probable next step (new role, new manager, new organization) you'll want to ensure you aren't jumping from the proverbial pan to the fire. If you decide a move is needed, be prepared to avoid the same, or worse, circumstances in the future.

The best way to make an informed decision is by researching the role, the hiring manager, and the company; and asking targeted questions in the job interview. I will provide additional guidance and examples of this under "How to Wow Interviewers."

Asking targeted questions will help you gain a clear sense of the role, your potential manager, and the workplace culture as they relate to your values. For example, if one of your top values is autonomy and you reported to a micromanager in the past, you could ask the hiring manager some of these sample questions in the interview to better understand her management style:

- How would your team describe your directing and delegation style?
- Would you describe the culture of the team and ways you've intentionally shaped the culture?
- Would you describe your approach and frequency for providing performance feedback?
- What is a setback or difficulty your team experienced and how did you lead your team through it?
- How do you communicate your expectations to your employees to ensure they are met?

If you're self-employed, consider the kinds of questions you might ask on a client questionnaire to determine if a prospect is a high value potential client, which you will need to define.

Use Google or the search engine of your preference to obtain ideas for interview questions that help uncover each non-negotiable value for you in the workplace. For example, search "Job interview questions to determine company culture."

When considering your values in decision making, you'll gain clarity on what is right for you and approach your decisions with increased confidence. You'll also increase the chances that your decision is best for your current and future happiness and satisfaction.

Do not skip assessing the fit of your values when searching for a new role. You can find a position that fits your strengths, skills, and interests, but if it violates your values the new job will be unsustainable, and Stein's law says anything that cannot continue must stop. Values violations never end well.

My Values Insights

What new understanding did you discover, or affirm, after completing your values exercise and reflecting on the questions provided?

Capture your insights:

_____

_____

_____

_____

_____

_____

_____

_____

_____

_____

_____

_____

_____

_____

_____

_____

_____

_____

_____

_____

_____

_____

I will go into greater detail in section two, "Blaze Your Path" about the practical application of using your values information to identify best fit roles. If you haven't already, you can download the values exercise at MyYouMap.com.

Discover Your Motivated Skills

"A winner is someone who recognizes his God-given talents, works his tail off to develop them into skills, and uses these skills to accomplish his goals."
— Larry Bird, Former NBA Basketball Player

The third pillar of career satisfaction is enjoying and being good at the skills you use daily in your work.

Nancy was a special needs teacher and assuredly made for this special calling. She loved teaching, encouraging, motivating, entertaining, listening, and dealing with her students' feelings. However, over time, the job became increasingly burdened with administrative work such as reporting, documenting, and maintaining records.

Despite her enjoyment of helping special needs kids, Nancy decided to leave because the administrative burdens of the role continued to expand and were too much to tolerate.

Nancy's job no longer aligned with her motivating skills because of the administrative red tape.

To review, skills fall into four categories:

Motivated Skills – Skills you're good at and enjoy doing consistently. For example, you might love conceptualizing, dealing with ambiguity, or working with numbers.

Burnout Skills – Skills you're good at, but *do not enjoy* doing regularly. For example, you might be proficient at working with numbers but find it tedious and draining.

Developmental Skills – Skills you would like to do more but haven't had an opportunity to develop, such as managing others. Perhaps you love managing your home budget but haven't had a chance with budget responsibility at work.

Low Priority Skills – Skills that no matter how much time you invest you don't seem to significantly improve your skill level. That's OK because you don't like to do them, either!

Your goal should be to attract motivated and developmental skills and avoid or reduce burn out and low priority skills.

You can either purchase a Knowdell Motivated Skills Sort online at www.careerplanner.com under "Career Tools for Individuals" to assess your skill interests or use the manual exercise provided below to clarify your motivated skills. The cost of the motivated skills online sort is under US$15. If you prefer to identify your motivated skills manually, you can review the list of fifty-two common skills provided below or download the exercise at MyYouMap.com.

Manual Skills Identification

Instructions: Review the following fifty-two skills and their corresponding definitions.

Check all skills you think you would enjoy consistently performing at work.

- Act as Liaison – Represent, serve as a link between individuals or groups
- Adapt to Change – Easily and quickly respond to changing assignments, work settings and priorities
- Ambiguity (Deal with) – Be comfortable and effective with issues that lack clarity, structure, or certainty
- Analyze – Break down and figure out problems logically
- Budget – Economize, save, stretch money or other resources
- Classify – Group, categorize, systematize data, people, or things
- Computer Literate – Develop, organize, complete tasks/projects using software: Word, Excel, PowerPoint
- Conceptualize – Conceive and internally develop concepts and ideas
- Counsel – Facilitate insight and personal growth, guide, advise, coach students, employees, or clients
- Customer Service – Effectively solve problems and challenges to satisfy

customers

- Deal with Feelings – Listen, accept, empathize, show sensitivity, defuse anger, use humor, appreciate
- Delegate – Achieve effective results by assigning tasks to others
- Design – Structure new or innovative practices, programs, products or environments
- Entertain/Perform – Amuse, sing, dance, create art, play music for, demonstrate or speak to an audience
- Estimating – Appraise value or cost
- Evaluate – Assess, review, or critique feasibility or quality
- Expedite – Speed up production or services, troubleshoot problems, streamline procedures
- Ideas (Generate) – Reflect upon, conceive of, dream up, brainstorm ideas
- Initiate Change – Exert influence to change status quo, exercise leadership to bring about new direction
- Implement – Provide detailed follow-through of policies and plans
- Improvise – To effectively think, speak, and act without preparation
- Innovate/Invent – Create unique ideas or combine existing ideas to obtain a new or unique result
- Interview for Information – Draw out subjects through insightful questioning
- Leadership – Organizing, motivating, providing direction to a group of people to achieve a common goal
- Maintain Records – Keep accurate and up-to-date records, log, record, itemize, collate, tabulate data
- Make Arrangements – Coordinate events and handle logistics
- Make Decisions – Make major, complex, or frequent decisions
- Manage Time – Ability to prioritize, structure and schedule tasks to maximize effort and meet deadlines
- Mentor – Educate, guide, coach, or counsel a less accomplished or junior colleague
- Mediate – Manage conflict and reconcile differences
- Monitor – Keep track of the movement of data, people, and things
- Motivate – Recruit involvement, mobilize energy, stimulate peak performance

- Multi-task – Effectively manage a variety of tasks and projects simultaneously
- Negotiate – Bargain for rights or advantages
- Numbers (Work with) – Calculate, compute, understand, solve numerical/quantitative problems
- Observe – Study, scrutinize, examine data, people or things, scientifically.
- Perceive Intuitively – Sense, show insight, and foresight
- Plan/Organize – Define goals and objectives, schedule and develop projects or programs
- Portray Images – Sketch, draw, illustrate, paint, photograph
- Proofread/Edit – Check writing for proper usage and stylistic flair, make improvements
- Read for Information – Research written resources efficiently and exhaustively
- Research Online – Use search engines on the Internet to gather and organize information and data
- Sell – Promote a person, company, goods or services, convince of merits, raise money
- Supervise – Oversee and direct the work of others
- Synthesize – Integrate ideas and information, combine diverse elements into a coherent whole
- Teach/Train – Inform, explain, give instruction to students, employees, or customers
- Team Work – Easily and effectively work with others to obtain results
- Test – Measure proficiency, quality, or validity, check and double check
- Use Mechanical Abilities – Assemble, tune, repair, or operate engines or other machinery
- Visualize – Imagine possibility, see in "mind's eye"
- Write – Compose reports, letters, articles, ads, stories, or educational materials

Skill Theme Identification

The same fifty-two skills are listed again below, this time grouped by skill relatedness, or category, such as Administrative, Leadership, and Interpersonal skills.

At this point, you should have finished selecting your motivated skills. Now, transfer your motivated skills to the table below by underlining or highlighting.

After you're done transferring each motivated skill under the categories below, observe where your motivated skills are predominantly themed and write down your top three categories.

I intentionally did not display skills according to category during the initial selection exercise above to avoid the category influencing the skills you chose to highlight. For example, if you're a people manager, you could be tempted to highlight the skills under Supervise because you felt you should.

SKILLS BY CATEGORY

Administrative
- Budget
- Classify
- Maintain Records

Artistic & Mechanical
- Entertain/Perform
- Portray Images
- Use Mechanical Abilities

Conceptual & Creative
- Ambiguity (Deal with)
- Conceptualize
- Design
- Ideas (Generate)
- Improvise
- Innovate/Invent
- Strategize
- Synthesize
- Visualize

Interpersonal
- Act as Liaison
- Counsel
- Deal with Feelings
- Mediate
- Perceive Intuitively
- Teach/Train
- Teamwork

Manage Process & Projects
- Adapt to Change
- Customer Service
- Expedite
- Implement
- Make Arrangements
- Manage Time
- Monitor
- Multitask
- Plan/Organize

Research & Analysis
- Analyze
- Evaluate
- Interview for Information
- Observe
- Read for Information
- Research Online

Sales
- Negotiate
- Sell

Supervisory
- Decision Making
- Delegate
- Supervise

Leadership
- Initiate Change
- Leadership
- Mentor
- Motivate

Technical & Information
- Computer Literacy
- Estimating
- Numbers (Work with)
- Proofread/Edit
- Test
- Write

My Motivated Skills Insights

What do you notice about where your motivated skills are themed? Are you surprised by the results? Do these skills and their corresponding categories reflect the requirements of your current or most recent role? If you're considering a career transition, how do your motivated skills align with careers you're considering?

Capture your insights:

_____

_____

_____

_____

_____

_____

_____

_____

_____

_____

_____

_____

_____

_____

A Word on Transferable Skills

Recently, I read survey results from a Harris poll conducted for the University of Phoenix. In that poll, a staggering 86% of workers in their twenties said they wanted to change careers, followed by 66% of those in their thirties, and 60% in their forties. Despite most workers having career plans in earlier years, 73% said they did not land in the career they expected.

With so many people desiring a career change, the ability to identify and communicate transferable skills is crucial. Regardless of role, many employers seek several key skills:

- Meeting deadlines
- Solving problems
- Organizing and managing projects
- Managing people
- Negotiation skills
- Computer skills
- Speaking in public
- Effective writing
- Managing budgets
- Customer focus

Korn Ferry reports that 85% **of skills are transferable** from job to job and only 15% of skills are specific to a role. For example, Bryan was a financial advisor who temporarily transitioned to a math teacher and then transitioned again into a desired role as a regional sales manager at a utilities company.

While a financial advisor and a regional sales manager at a utility company are in different industries and might not seem related, they are. Both jobs involve relationship building, persuading others, communicating ideas, strategic planning, marketing, account management, new business development, client relationship management, building rapport, being results-driven, solving problems, listening, creating customer solutions, and providing customer service.

The biggest obstacle that prevents people from seeing skills as portable is binding industry jargon to one's skills. I frequently see people do this on their resumes. They include all the industry-specific language that prevents a skill from being perceived as stand-alone. Transferable. When you strip away the unnecessary industry lingo, a skill is a skill. Don't believe me? Check this out:

This was one of Bryan's resume bullets before:

> Built and managed all aspects of a 65-million-dollar book of business consisting of individual, retirement, qualified plan, nonprofit and foundation assets. This included client communication, individual stock and bond selection, mutual fund analysis and selection, separate account manager due diligence and selection, pricing of advisory services, supervision of sales assistant, development and review of new business acquisition plan.

This was the same resume bullet with industry jargon removed:

> Built and managed all aspects of a national $65 million book of business; included account management, client communications, development and review of new business acquisition plan, pricing, and supervision of sales staff.

Can you see how the former bullet would be a turn-off when trying to transition to a new role or industry, while the latter uses familiar and accessible language, regardless of industry?

Resumes will be covered later in "Show the World!", but I want to drive home the point that your skills are far more transferable than you think! I will go into more depth in "Blaze Your Path" on the practical application of using your motivated skills to identify best fit roles.

Discover How You're Wired

"There is an amazing power getting to know your inner self and learning how to use it and not fight with the world. If you know what makes you happy, your personality, interests and capabilities; just use them, and everything else flows beautifully." – Juhi Chawla, Actress

The fourth pillar of career satisfaction is your personality-based interests. I could have used the term personality for the fourth pillar of career satisfaction. However, I opted instead to concentrate on the career application of personality: How our personality, or "wiring", influences career interests. I use the terms "wired" and "interests" interchangeably throughout this book with the understanding that these concepts are influenced by personality.

I met Luis, a true creative, in 2016. He had been working a routine job while his heartfelt interests were expressing creativity and having an impact on people. He told me he felt like a cork bobbing in the ocean and had completely lost sight of who he was. Luis's problem was his work didn't align with how he was wired, or his interests.

A discovery process prevalent in both research and practice is the personality-based Holland Occupational Themes named after American psychologist John Holland. His career interest research is also referred to as Holland's Theory of Career Choice. Each person is inspired differently, from an interest point of view, depending on which personality pattern he or she identifies with.

In Holland's book, Making Vocational Choices: A Theory of Careers, he also argues that "a six-category scheme built on the assumption that there are only six kinds of people in the world is unacceptable on the strength of common sense alone, but a six-category scheme that allows a simple ordering of a person's resemblance to each of the six models provides the possibility of seven-hundred-twenty different personality patterns."

Holland's six core interest types are:

Realistic – The Doers
Investigative – The Thinkers
Artistic – The Creators
Social – The Helpers
Enterprising – The Persuaders
Conventional – The Organizers

Following is a high-level overview of the six career interest types.

Realistic – The Doers

Individuals with a Realistic career code tend to prefer work that involves practical, hands-on solutions to problems. They value things they can see, touch, and use. Realistic types would rather work with their hands than sit behind a desk. Many, but not all, Realistic occupations work outside and possibly deal with machinery, tools, or animals and don't involve much paperwork.

Sample occupations: ambulance drivers, EMTs, firefighters, security guards, technicians, veterinarians, environmental engineers, and electricians

Investigative – The Thinkers

Those with an Investigative career code are intellectual, curious, and reserved. They like to solve problems and engage in challenges. Investigative types do not like routine work that forces them to check their brain at the door. In fact, their work often involves ideas and heavy mental lifting. They also tend to avoid careers that involve leading or influencing people and selling.

Sample occupations: fire investigators, registered nurses, nuclear medicine technologists, software developers, business intelligence analysts, biostatisticians, market research analysts, and database architects

Artistic – The Creators

People with an Artistic career code are imaginative, creative, original, independent, and expressive. In general, they tend to avoid work that involves highly structured or routine activities. These individuals are inspired to create, whether through activities such as music, writing, drawing, dance, photography, or art.

Sample occupations: chefs, fashion designers, graphic artists, interior designers, sound engineering technicians, landscape architects, authors, and technical writers

Social – The Helpers

Individuals with a Social career code are interested in serving society and making a difference in people's lives. They like to help people, and their work is most often centered around people. Those interested in Social careers, particularly when it's an individual's primary code, often gravitate toward nonprofit organizations, education, healthcare, and social work. They are helpful, friendly, loyal, generous, and trustworthy.

Sample occupations: counseling psychologists, health educators, patient representatives, psychology teachers, midwives, dietetic technicians, teacher assistants, and social workers

Enterprising – The Persuaders

Enterprising individuals often deal with business, leadership, or politics and are involved in making decisions, starting up and carrying out projects, and selling ideas or things. Enterprising types are generally energetic, ambitious, dominant, outgoing, and competitive.

Sample occupations: financial services, sales representatives, chief executives (CEO, COO, EVP), judges, education administrators, supply chain managers, and human resources specialists

Conventional – The Organizers

Conventional career types are the glue that hold an organization together. They provide the structure, process, and order that organizations need to run effectively. People with this career type are generally methodical, detail-oriented, cautious, organized, responsible, and quality-oriented.

Sample occupations: insurance claim clerks, medical secretaries, accountants, pharmacy technicians, loan officers, research assistants, information security analysts, and financial analysts

These six career types provide a glimpse into a person's internal, interpersonal, and environmental preferences. Once we hone in on the two strongest career types, more specific preferences are revealed.

After reading the descriptions for each of the six career interest types, which of them do you identify with most? When helping people with career exploration, I use one of two free online interest profilers to discover a person's occupational interest type, found here:

The O*NET Interest Profiler – www.mynextmove.org/explore/ip
The Career Aptitude Test at 123 Test – www.123test.com/career-test

You can take both assessments to determine which one returns a result that appears most like you.

Take a moment, now, to discover your career interest type by taking one or both career interest assessments. Each career interest test should take about five minutes. The tests also provide sample occupations that match your career interest type. Think of these as prototypes or patterns of career fit, rather than firm recommendations.

Are you surprised by your results? Revisit the definitions above for your primary and secondary codes.

Following are thirty career types derived from all the possible primary and secondary code combinations.

The source of these career type descriptions is Jan Lowe and Tracy Lungrin's book, CareerCode: Know Your Code, Find Your Fit (2014). To read about your career type in detail, consider purchasing a copy of this book. CareerCode is a must-have resource for career services professionals.

Artistic + Conventional (The Creator and The Organizer) – The Critic

Descriptors: picky, methodical, sharp-tongued, protective, technical, temperamental, perceptive and accurate, cultivated, complex, controversial, clever. *Picture yourself as a Critic.*

The Critic has a desire to create or experience works that illuminate the human condition but also wants to see it done right.

Artistic + Enterprising (The Creator and The Persuader) – The Performer

Descriptors: big spender, great storyteller, the center of attention, conceptual, resourceful, dramatic, charismatic, easily bored, idealistic, impatient, impulsive, eternally optimistic. *Picture yourself in Advertising.*

The Performer likes to interact with an audience, actively presenting his or her talent, whether through public speaking, directing, producing, or performing.

Artistic + Investigative (The Creator and The Thinker) – The Idealist

Descriptors: intensely verbal, private, opinionated, well-read, somewhat antisocial, highly idealistic, perpetually thinking, intolerant of mundane people, extremely perceptive. *Picture yourself as an Author.*

The Idealist is most fascinated by the work in his or her head, exploring ideas, and creating.

Artistic + Realistic (The Creator and The Doer) – The Designer

Descriptors: visionary, sensitive, inventive, argumentative, meticulous, patient with the artistic process, lover of architecture, into photography, introverted, original, internally focused. *Picture yourself as a Graphic Designer.*

The Designer needs an artistic outlet to be fulfilled by working with something tactile or visual.

Artistic + Social (The Creator and The Helper) – The Nurturer

Descriptors: Bohemian, concerned about the environment, empathetic, accepting of other people, cultures, and attitudes; a free spirit; a little spacey; good-hearted; holistic; a music lover; and noncompetitive. *Picture yourself as an Art Teacher.*

The Nurturer needs creative stimulation and flexibility to work with others in a creative way.

Conventional + Artistic (The Organizer and The Creator) – The Curator

Descriptors: great homemaker, perfectionist, precise, impatient, good at pulling things together, interested in structure, anxious, traditional, organized, pressed, neat and clean, proper. *Picture yourself as a Historical Librarian.*

The Curator likes rules, systems, and procedures applied to beauty, creativity, or art. They are interested in collections. A combination with an orientation to both order and creativity is unusual.

Conventional + Enterprising (The Organizer and The Persuader) – The Regulator

Descriptors: highly accurate, disciplined, industrious, focused, a governor, anal-retentive, a recognition seeker, pushy, reliable, responsible and trustworthy; honest; tightly wound. *Picture yourself as a Government Regulator.*

The Regulator likes the challenge of entering a fresh situation, figuring it out, and finding flaws to fix so things run smoothly.

Conventional + Investigative (The Organizer and The Thinker) – The Analyst

Descriptors: attentive, cautious, contentious, deliberate, meticulous, judgmental, persistent, self-disciplined, reserved, and stable. *Picture yourself as a Budget Analyst.*

The Analyst tends to do best in roles with clearly defined projects, preferably involving numbers, code, or data.

Conventional + Realistic (The Organizer and The Doer) – The Inspector

Descriptors: rule follower, obedient, concrete, orderly and organized, steady and focused, predictable, structured, dependable, repetitive, stable, detail-oriented, confrontational. *Picture yourself as an Auditor.*

The Inspector needs order and careful planning. They thrive on predictability and routine.

Conventional + Social (The Organizer and The Helper) – The Coordinator

Descriptors: Puts systems in place, detail-oriented, shows people around, efficient, moral, obedient, organized, precise, scheduled, structured, helpful, something of a martyr (will feel responsible for the whole world if not careful). *Picture yourself in a College Admissions Office.*

The Coordinator desires positive, helpful interactions with people where basic courtesy is valued.

Enterprising + Artistic (The Persuader and The Creator) – The Promoter

Descriptors: natural marketer, ambitious, slightly arrogant, charismatic, visionary, competitive, idealistic, expressive, high-energy, boisterous, rule bender, initiative taker. *Picture yourself as a Producer.*

The Promoter enjoys being a part of artistic productions and bold new projects. Entertaining, publishing, fashion, and other artistic projects are where this career type will feel most satisfied.

Enterprising + Conventional (The Persuader and The Organizer) – The Director

Descriptors: business-minded, competitive, workaholic, managerial (can get the most out of people), efficient, excellent time manager, intense, successful, take-charge, a taskmaster). *Picture yourself as the Manager of an Insurance Agency.*

The Director needs the authority to direct and make decisions. This career type likes to achieve through planning and follow-through.

Enterprising + Investigative (The Persuader and The Thinker) – The Strategist

Descriptors: visionary, ambitious, planner, demanding, agenda-oriented, logical, organized, persuasive, self-confident, take-charge, slightly abrasive at times, a salesperson, an executer. *Picture yourself as a Corporate Strategist.*

The Strategist likes to be in control, challenged, and appreciated. The freedom to pursue his or her ideas, in their own way, is important.

Enterprising + Realistic (The Persuader and The Doer) – The Broker

Descriptors: born leader, powerful negotiator, great salesperson, influential and blunt, forceful, power seeker, workaholic, confrontational, confident, and courageous. *Picture yourself as a Broker.*

The Broker seeks to be in control and likes to get out and make things happen independently. Collaboration isn't really the Broker's style.

Enterprising + Social (The Persuader and The Helper) – The Ambassador

Descriptors: diplomatic, mover and shaker, overextended (take on more than you have time for when people need your help), great communicator, popular, resourceful, talented soft seller, glad hander (can work a room), relationship-centered, community-oriented. *Picture yourself as a Politician.*

The Ambassador needs to be on the go, making connections, and working the crowd. This person needs to do things his or her way.

Investigative Career Types

Investigative + Artistic (The Thinker and The Creator) – The Scholar

Descriptors: highly observant, deep thinker, intuitive, insightful, complex, researcher, introverted, intellectual, independent, opinionated. *Picture yourself as a Sociologist.*

The Scholar is an original thinker, driven by the investigation of ideas and connections between things.

Investigative + Conventional (The Thinker and The Organizer) – The Examiner

Descriptors: systematic thinker, accurate, anal-retentive, cautious, critical, no fan of surprises, deeply engaged with whatever they do, quick with calculations, opinionated, precise, uncompromising. *Picture yourself as an Actuary.*

The Examiner enjoys systematic work in the form of clearly defined projects he or she can follow through to completion.

Investigative + Enterprising (The Thinker and The Persuader) – The Innovator

Descriptors: competent, critical thinker, curious, expert, persuasive, systems thinker, opinionated, strategic, entrepreneurial, competitive, sharp. *Picture yourself as a Technical Consultant.*

The Innovator likes a variety of projects and opportunities to follow where ideas lead. Following strict procedures will be a bad match.

Investigative + Realistic (The Thinker and The Doer) – The Scientist

Descriptors: scientific, logical, analytical, mathematical, highly intelligent, avid reader, very curious, inquisitive, and critical. *Picture yourself as a Biologist.*

The Scientist needs work that stimulates the mind, sufficient autonomy, and a chance to contribute to the expansion of knowledge.

Investigative + Social (The Thinker and The Helper) – The Practitioner

Descriptors: caring, diagnostic, cautious, curious, analytical, overextended (take on more than you have time for when people need your help), independent, intellectual, objective, introverted. *Picture yourself as a Health Practitioner.*

The Practitioner is bored by repetitive tasks and wants to do work that makes a difference. He or she likes to help others by figuring out and solving their problems.

Realistic Career Types

Realistic + Artistic (The Doer and The Creator) – The Crafter

Descriptors: project-focused, into patterns, interested in restoration and repair, perfectionist, introverted, self-reliant, minimalist, tenacious, resourceful. *Picture yourself as an Artisan.*

The Crafter desires getting lost in projects that require using his or her hands, creating things that serve a function or make the world brighter.

Realistic + Conventional (The Doer and The Organizer) – The Technician

Descriptors: precise, careful, hands-on, into routine, task-oriented, efficient, persistent, reserved, intense, mechanically-minded. *Picture yourself as a Service Technician.*

The Technician requires a degree of independence while working on physical projects like repairing or installing.

Realistic + Enterprising (The Doer and The Persuader) – The Sergeant

Descriptors: natural supervisor, dependable, opinionated, aggressive, autocratic, self-starter, motivator, determined, stubborn, hard worker, temperamental. *Picture yourself as a Construction Foreman.*

The Sergeant likes to be in the thick of the action, but that action must have a mission, clear objectives, and measurable outcomes.

Realistic + Investigative (The Doer and The Thinker) – The Engineer

Descriptors: methodical, diligent, strict (Close enough isn't in your vocabulary.), thrifty, introverted at times, critical (Work that doesn't meet your standards gets on your nerves.), rational, hard on yourself, gadget/technology-oriented. *Picture yourself as an Engineer.*

The Engineer is driven to gather specialized information and use it to solve problems.

Realistic + Social (The Doer and The Helper) – The Attendant

Descriptors: dependable, fraternal, busy, problem solver, facilitator, community-oriented, athletic, helpful, practical, hands-on, responsive. *Picture yourself as a Physical Therapist.*

The Attendant must work with people, producing tangible results to help others.

Social Career Types

Social + Artistic (The Helper and The Creator) – The Advocate

Descriptors: talkative, positive thinker, absentminded, trusting, forgiving, warm, hospitable, accepting, giving, sensitive, vulnerable. *Picture yourself as a Nonprofit Worker.*

The Advocate needs a flexible and relaxed work environment where he or she can make a difference and get to know people without strict deadline and productivity pressures.

Social + Conventional (The Helper and The Organizer) – The Caretaker

Descriptors: team player, good communicator, responsible and dependable; helpful; loyal; fan of order; reliable; respectful of authority; trustworthy; hospitable. *Picture yourself as a Case Worker.*

The Caretaker works best with clearly defined protocols and expectations. They are generally not well suited for management positions where they are expected to set the standards and deal with unforeseen circumstances.

Social + Enterprising (The Helper and The Persuader) – The Connector

Descriptors: community-minded, guide (You love showing visitors around.), facilitator, friendly and outgoing; a sharer; averse to confrontation; good listener; problem solver, understanding. *Picture yourself as a Community Relations Coordinator.*

The Connector is among the most outgoing people of all. They want to interact with people as their equal to solve meaningful problems.

Social + Investigative (The Helper and The Thinker) – The Specialist

Descriptors: responsible, helpful, insightful, concerned, supportive, rational, tactful, understanding, perceptive, inquisitive, systematic, team player. *Picture yourself as a School Psychologist.*

The Specialist seeks a purposeful career, usually in a helping profession. They do not enjoy simply socializing with people but want to learn about them in a way that provides intellectual stimulation.

Social + Realistic (The Helper and The Doer) – The Trainer

Descriptors: coach, mentor, team player, social, doer, competitive, persistent, responsible, goal-oriented. *Picture yourself as a Director of Recreation.*

The Trainer likes to work with others as a team, promoting a sense of community for the common good.

If your second and third career types are scored within one or two percent of each other in your career test results, it's possible that two career type options might be representative of you. The image below contains results from the 123 Career Test for a client who had a primary career interest type of Conventional (27%). However, notice how the client's secondary and tertiary interest types (Social and Investigative) are tied at 20%.

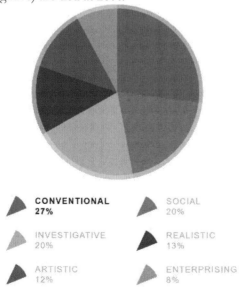

	CONVENTIONAL 27%		SOCIAL 20%
	INVESTIGATIVE 20%		REALISTIC 13%
	ARTISTIC 12%		ENTERPRISING 8%

Because of the second-place tie between Social and Investigative, my client had to consider which career type best represented her:

The Coordinator (Conventional/Social): The Organizer and The Helper—a person who likes to create structure and help others.

The Analyst (Conventional/Investigative): The Organizer and The Thinker—a person who enjoys creating structure and solving complex challenges and problems.

After reviewing the two different definitions, my client determined that the Conventional/Investigative career type, The Analyst, best explained her overall approach to work. However, because she enjoys mentoring and investing in people, she felt the Conventional/Social type, The Coordinator, best explained her from an interpersonal point of view.

Interestingly, this client is an introvert who loves creating and improving processes—very typical for a Conventional—but she also enjoys organizing events to bring people together, such as lunch and learns. This is atypical for a Conventional/Investigative, but characteristic of the Conventional/Social.

People are nuanced and complex!

In addition to your first two interest codes, pay attention to the last two codes in your six-letter chain. They are rank ordered. Therefore, the final two codes are your weakest career interest. For example, if an individual has a career code of IAECRS, the sixth code of S, Social, indicates a career in social services is not going to fit.

Another example is a person whose sixth code is C, Conventional. He or she should avoid careers that require strict rules, deadlines, and structure.

Use the space below to capture your thoughts about your career interest results and some of the descriptive words that you think accurately describe you. If you aren't certain the results you received reflect you, I recommend taking the test again and comparing your results.

Capture your insights:

_____

_____

_____

_____

_____

_____

_____

_____

_____

_____

_____

_____

_____

In section two, "Blaze Your Path," I will delve into using your career interest type to identify and research roles. I will also provide a more detailed overview of the O*NET Career Interest Profiler.

Before we begin the process of creating your personalized YouMap®, permit me to take a brief detour to recommend an additional assessment resource if you are a student or the parent of a student between the ages of 12 and 22, The SchoolPlace Big Five Profile™.

Calling All Students!

I first became certified in the SchoolPlace Big Five Profile™—as well as the adult version called The WorkPlace Big Five Profile™—back in 2012 and was recently certified as a Master Trainer in both.

Paradigm Personality Labs (formerly The Center for Applied Cognitive Studies) is the creator of the SchoolPlace Big Five Profile™ and describes it as follows:

> "The SchoolPlace assessment and reports, formulated specifically for the academic environment, help students build self-awareness and understand their strengths and weaknesses as they relate to school and future careers. Students who are more in touch with themselves are better equipped to figure out which career paths are right for them."

While the YouMap® is an effective tool for students, the SchoolPlace Big Five Profile™ assessment is an excellent supplement to the process because it provides additional insight into specific behavioral traits that younger adults and students might not be acutely aware of.

Increased self-awareness is one of the top predictors of career success, according to results of a 2006 study by Accenture, and another study published in the Journal of Organizational Behavior in 2003, "Predictors of success in the era of the boundaryless career."

The SchoolPlace Big Five Profile™ measures five "super-traits" and twenty-three individual "sub-traits" based on the Five-Factor Model of personality and is backed by more than twenty years of psychological research.

The five super-traits and the corresponding sub-traits that describe school-related behavior are:

Need for Stability (N)
Explains how young people respond to and handle stressful situations

The sub-traits:
- Worry
- Temper
- Outlook
- Coping Level

Extroversion (E)
Explains the degree to which one enjoys being in the thick of the action

The sub-traits:
- Approach level
- Group orientation
- Pace
- Leadership
- Trust
- Tact

Originality (O)
Explains the degree to which one is open to new things

The sub-traits:

- Imagination
- Range of interests
- Innovation
- Zoom Scale (Level of detail-orientation)

Accommodation (A)
The degree to which someone accommodates others

The sub-traits:
- Service (to others)
- Compliance
- Humility
- Speaking out level

Consolidation (C)
Explains the degree to which one pushes toward goals

The sub-traits:
- Thoroughness
- Structure
- Ambition
- Concentration
- Methodicalness

Ian's Story

I first met Ian and his father in 2015 when I was facilitating a career workshop in South Carolina for job seekers. After the workshop, Ian's dad approached me and asked for my contact information.

Ian had spent the past year in culinary school and had recently dropped out of the program. His parents were perplexed because Ian loved to cook and was good at it. He often prepared new meal creations at home for his family.

What went wrong?

At that point, they were at a complete loss to understand how a role that fit both Ian's interests and natural talents went wrong. I administered the assessment to Ian and met with him and his parents to review the results.

Four specific insights surfaced to explain why the culinary field was a poor fit for Ian:

- A need to always plan, rather than work spontaneously
- A tendency to concentrate and not multi-task
- High perfectionism
- A worrier who is sensitive to stress

Picture how Ian must have felt in a restaurant kitchen; a hectic environment that requires a thinking on the fly, multi-tasking, and is highly stressful. The environment at home was quite different because it was absent the stress or pressure to multi-task.

Ian ended up studying design, which matches his strengths, motivating skills, and interests but is more aligned with his behavioral tendencies. The last time I spoke to Ian's father, he told me Ian was thriving and couldn't be happier.

If you would like to increase your awareness of your behavioral tendencies, or you are the parent of a student, the SchoolPlace and WorkPlace Big Five Profile™ are excellent assessments to consider.

The YouMap® Career Profile

Once you've identified and confirmed your four pillars of career fulfillment (strengths, values, motivating skills and how your interests are wired) you will have a strong foundation for building your unique contribution statement, also known as your value proposition. Your value proposition will be the starting point to targeting your next step for your career in section two, "Blaze Your Path."

In 2017, I collaborated with graphic designer and branding specialist, Crystal Davies, of Davies Designs, to create The YouMap®.

The YouMap® is a summarized report of your strengths, values, motivating skills, and career interests. YouMap® is also a one-page branding document that offers a place to include your unique contribution statement.

This branding document is an excellent resource you can use to compare opportunities against your strengths, values, skills, and interests. Equally important, it can be used as a powerful marketing tool to bring to a job interview. You bet interviewers will be impressed! (My clients say so.)

A sample one-page summary of the YouMap® career profile is shown here.

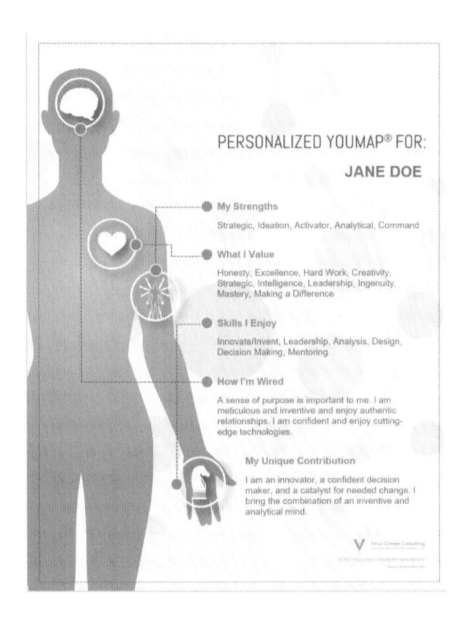

PERSONALIZED YOUMAP® FOR:

JANE DOE

My Strengths

Strategic, Ideation, Activator, Analytical, Command

What I Value

Honesty, Excellence, Hard Work, Creativity,
Strategic, Intelligence, Leadership, Ingenuity,
Mastery, Making a Difference

Skills I Enjoy

Innovate/Invent, Leadership, Analysis, Design,
Decision Making, Mentoring

How I'm Wired

A sense of purpose is important to me. I am
meticulous and inventive and enjoy authentic
relationships. I am confident and enjoy cutting-
edge technologies.

My Unique Contribution

I am an innovator, a confident decision
maker, and a catalyst for needed change. I
bring the combination of an inventive and
analytical mind.

Create Your Own YouMap® Career Profile

Do you remember Anna, my accounting manager client I introduced at the beginning of the book? After we completed her YouMap®, it became clear that Anna was not in the wrong profession; she was in the wrong environment.

Many clients have contacted me ready to scrap their career and pivot in a new direction. You might find, like Anna did, that your greatest drivers of career dissatisfaction are not at the role level—they are at the manager or company level.

Specifically, Anna's manager and workplace culture violated her value of continuous improvement because they were happy to ignore or patch up problems rather than fix them. She also had Developer as a strength—the natural mentor, trainer, coach, and teacher—yet her manager would tell her to stop spending time investing in people through mentoring and training. That was troubling to her.

I'm happy to report Anna found a better job! She wrote me an email saying, "Lots of values alignment at the new company. Yay! Thank you for helping me figure out what wasn't working where I was and what I value!"

I first met Deana in 2013. She quit her job as a marketing manager without another job lined up and felt horribly guilty. She told me she felt she let her family down. She decided to get out of marketing after eight years. After working together, we identified her career dissatisfaction was unrelated to marketing. Rather, the problem was trying to lead marketing in her organization's culture.

For starters, none of the executive leadership team were on the same page with their strategic marketing goals, which pulled Deana and her team in multiple directions. She had no Influencing strengths, so fighting to get her voice heard and constantly shielding her team from the resource conflict was stressful.

Additionally, she had Belief in her Top 5 strengths (strong core values that guide one's life), and the organization participated in some less-than-honest business practices. The complete and utter violation of her core values that stemmed from her Belief strength made the situation untenable. She couldn't stay. She was ready to throw eight years of experience out the window when she just needed to perform her role elsewhere.

Therefore, as you complete your own personalized YouMap®, remember to consider if your values and strengths could be leveraged somewhere else in the same field. However, if the skills of your job would be similar regardless of where you work, and you don't enjoy doing them, a role change is in order.

Now, are you ready for the most exciting step of the "Find Yourself" section?

A simplified YouMap® template is provided as a download to allow you to enter the information from your assessments and exercises in each of the four discovery sections: strengths, values, motivated skills, and how you're wired (personality-based career interests). Go to MyYouMap.com to download your own YouMap® template.

Enter your results into the YouMap® template as follows:

1. Add your Top 5 strengths from the Clifton StrengthsFinder into the first section of the template, "My Strengths."
2. Enter your 5-10 prioritized values into the next section, "What I Value."
3. List the skills you chose as motivating in the "Skills I Enjoy" section.
4. Enter your career interest type, and any words or phrases that describe you from the "Discover How You're Wired" part of the book, into the "How I'm Wired" section of the YouMap®.

Finally, read through your profile and reflect on your unique attributes. What do you do better than other people? What are some of the insights you can harness to summarize what you do best? This is your unique value contribution.

To complete your YouMap®, take a few minutes to craft a statement for the "My Unique Contribution" section. Select words and phrases from your strengths, values, or from the "How You're Wired" section of your YouMap®. Combine these phrases to best describe yourself in one or two sentences. Be prepared to back up your statement with an example when it comes time for an interview.

Tip: The "Strengths Insight Guide" you downloaded from the Gallup website when you completed the Clifton StrengthsFinder assessment is an excellent source of strengths-based language to describe you. You can combine these phrases with the outcome or result the strength produces—what an employer or client receives.

Here are some examples of "My Unique Contribution" statements:

> I possess an uncommon blend of strong process and people orientation.
> I enjoy solving problems and developing people toward increased performance.

> When working with clients, I tailor my approach to draw out and understand each client's unique needs. I am meticulous and tireless in bringing their vision to reality.

> My unique contribution is a rare trait of being analytical and methodical with a strong social orientation. This leads to a customer-centric approach to problem solving, strategy, planning, analysis and research, while fostering an environment of service and collaboration.

> I have an imaginative mind that generates novel ideas complimented by strategic practicality to identify the most viable and feasible options to solve problems or improve an outcome.

> I'm an independent and focused goal setter who thrives in dynamic environments and seeks continuous improvement and innovation. I am adept at planning and designing solutions.

Even if some of these unique contribution statements sound like you, do not copy and paste them into your YouMap®. Go through the exercise of jotting down key words and phrases from your profile to come up with a statement that strongly reflects you.

Once your profile is complete you can bring it with you to a job interview or share it with clients. I'll go into detail how to use your document during an interview in the "Show the World!" section.

If completing your YouMap® proves tricky or difficult, skip ahead to the section "Case Study: Antonette, The Pharma Sales Rep" immediately following the YouMap® template on the next page. I'll walk through a case study of an actual client and break down each step of the discovery process using my client's information. With her permission, I share insights about her results in each step to bring additional clarity to the process.

If you've completed your YouMap®, I recommend taking one additional step before we move to the next section of the book.

On your YouMap®, highlight your "deal makers" and "deal breakers" in each of the four pillars of career satisfaction that we've explored. Deal makers are the strengths, skills, values, and aspects of your career interests that you must have in your next role.

Deal breakers are the things you must avoid when considering a career move. Most often your deal breakers are found in your burnout skills. You simply don't want to take a position that will require you to perform certain skills on a regular basis.

Identifying your deal makers and deal breakers now can help you avoid compromising too much when looking to make a move. While no job is perfect or absent all tasks we dislike, identifying nonnegotiable factors will help you stay true to yourself when making decisions. In section two, "Blaze Your Path," you will put the results of this highlighting exercise into action.

A sample of the YouMap® is illustrated below. Again, you can download a copy at MyYouMap.com.

JANE DOE YOUMAP®

My Unique Contribution

I'm an innovator, a confident decision maker, and a catalyst for change.
I bring the combination of an inventive and analytical mind.

 Self-Assurance, Ideation, Activator, Restorative, Analytical

 Honesty, Contribution, Strategic Thinking, Community, Innovation, Belonging, Autonomy, Making a Difference, Personal Growth, Fun

 Strategy, Writing, Inventing, Delegation, Leadership, Design, Teamwork, Analysis, Research, Initiating Change, Mentoring, Conceptualizing, Visualizing

 The Designer: An original thinker driven by the investigation of ideas and connections between things. Highly observant and intuitive.

Case Study: Antonette, The Pharma Sales Rep

Let's review a real client case study to illustrate the power of the process that results in your YouMap®.

Antonette was a pharmaceutical sales representative whom I met in 2017. She had recently taken a bold risk and quit her job. In our first phone conversation, Antonette shared she has never landed in the right role, with the right manager, in the right company in her 25-year career. She knew something was missing, and most jobs felt very cookie cutter. They just didn't seem to fit her.

Antonette had taken strength and personality assessments in the past. However, the information had not been debriefed or organized into an integrated story until she went through the YouMap® career profile process with me.

The YouMap® revealed some surprising insights and equipped Antonette to articulate what was missing from her career up to that point. I'll present her case study using each of the pillars of career satisfaction, share the insights she gained, and show her final profile, highlighting the gaps in the career path she had pursued.

Antonette's Strengths

This table outlines Antonette's Driver, Passenger, and Fuel strengths. Take a moment to review.

DRIVER
Strategic (Thinking Theme) – You find alternative ways to proceed, sorting through clutter to find the best route. This skill cannot be taught. You play out alternative scenarios allowing you to see around the next corner. You discard paths that lead nowhere.
PASSENGERS
Achiever (Executing Theme) – You have a great deal of stamina and work hard. You take great satisfaction from being busy and productive. Your drive is the power supply that causes you to set the pace and define productivity levels for others. **Learner** (Thinking Theme) – You have a great desire to continuously improve. Learning enables you to thrive in dynamic work environments where you are asked to take on short project assignments and learn a lot about the new subject matter in a short period of time.
FUEL
Input (Thinking Theme) – You have a craving to know more and often collect and archive information. You keep acquiring, compiling and filing stuff away because it's interesting and keeps your mind fresh—without knowing when and why you might need it. **Futuristic** (Thinking Theme) – You are inspired by what could be and you inspire others with your vision. You see in detail what the future might hold, and it pulls you forward. You make the picture as vivid as possible for others to see and keep asking, "Wouldn't it be great if…."

Antonette's Strengths Insights

As a pharmaceutical sales representative, Antonette spent a lot of time on the road meeting with health care providers. Her job was characterized by the following responsibilities:

- Achieving aggressive sales targets in numbers-driven environments
- Cold calling to increase revenue and market share
- Executing sales strategies
- Influencing and persuading clients in high status positions, namely physicians

Following are three explanations why Antonette's strengths were not suited for sales:

Influencing without authority – Antonette has no Influencing themes in her Top 5 strengths. Therefore, she does not enjoy circumstances where she is expected to make things happen through influence and persuasion. Most sales people have one or more Influencing strengths.

Few intellectual challenges – Antonette's strengths are heavily represented in the Thinking category (four out of five), with one strength in the Executing category. She is a thinker/doer. Because of her large number of thinking themes, her role must require brain power, as she will quickly tire of work that is routine or not intellectually challenging. Sales is more relationship influence than intellectual challenge. (No, I'm not saying sales people don't think or like to use their brains!)

Insufficient learning opportunities – Learner is in Antonette's top strengths. Therefore, it's important for her to grow and learn new things on a consistent basis. Learners get wander lust after a role offers little opportunity to stretch themselves. Once she learned the ropes of her clients and territory, insufficient learning opportunities left her dissatisfied.

It became apparent in our first session that Antonette's strengths would be better suited in a role other than sales. Now, let's look at her values story.

Antonette's Values

Perhaps now might be a good time to stop and complete your values exercise, if you haven't already, and then read the insights from Antonette's case study. It's not required, but it will be helpful to have your list of values in front of you.

If you've completed a values assessment in the past, feel free to use those results. Take time to prioritize your values. The "Discover Your Values" section contains an exercise to reveal and prioritize your values and explains why prioritizing your values is important. You can download the values exercise at MyYouMap.com.

During our second session, Antonette and I discussed her values and what is most important to her. She had completed the values exercise, including prioritizing them, prior to our meeting.

Antonette created the following prioritized list of values. I have included her definitions of each value and her comments from the session.

ANTONETTE'S TOP VALUES

Dynamism – Movement, forward motion, incorporates doing something important and dynamic to move an idea or an organization forward.

Inner Harmony – I feel like I'm in the right place, at the right time, doing the right thing. FLOW! I don't have anxiety. I can feel peace inside. We're all together. I get a gnawing feeling when I'm asked to do something that feels like a lie or stretching the truth.

Commitment – Alignment and integrity. Commitment at the individual and team levels. Of one accord.

Vitality/Health – Is what I'm doing affirming life (not just my life but everybody I'm touching)? How happy am I about Monday coming around? Mental health is the biggest. Does the atmosphere provoke anxiety or fear? Time off, reasonable expectations, occasional work from home. A place that's flexible and progressive enough that a person's whole health is considered. For example, can I take a walk at lunch, or walk to work, standing desks, allow physical activity? Do they emphasize employee wellness?

Mastery – Excellence and beauty. I can appreciate when someone or a company is good at something, such as how they communicate to customers and employees. When I'm working with leaders, how do they demonstrate their mastery? Do they talk at you or get in the trenches with you? I learn better that way (in the trenches). It's a goal for me to get better.

Community/Service/Making a Difference/Love & Connection – I must make a difference. I can find community with like-minded people anywhere, but then when everyone is out for themselves I feel adrift. I'm usually someone who helps build community and make connections. I've got energy to be of service at work!

Antonette's Values Insights

Antonette and I reviewed her values, one at a time. Then I asked her three questions, which I discuss below.

What does dynamism [Value #1] mean to you?

It's critical to personally define a value. I don't care how Merriam-Webster's dictionary defines a word, I care what it means to you. As you can see from the illustration above, Antonette defined dynamism as "Movement, forward motion, incorporates doing something important and dynamic to move an idea or an organization forward."

Do you desire this value to be reciprocated in the workplace by your manager and/or team members?

Two of Antonette's values are reciprocal: Commitment, and Community/Service/Making a Difference/Love & Connection. Both were violated in her last role. Antonette shared that it was important to have a sense of alignment at the individual and team levels—to be of one accord. In a contract sales position, everyone tends to be out for themselves.

Was/Is this value honored or violated in your role, by your manager, and in the workplace culture?

When I asked Antonette if her role, manager, or company culture honored or violated her first value, Dynamism, she told me it was violated at the role level. She elaborated that her position was a contract role, which meant the only option was to do that role and then leave. In her words, "They don't need you to belong or be aligned. They just need you to do the job. You can sell any pill."

The ability to do something important, to move an idea or the organization forward in a temporary role wasn't in the cards, which left Antonette feeling disconnected and without purpose.

As with her strengths, Antonette's values were not aligned to her sales role. That's a two for two mismatch. Next, let's see what we discovered about her motivated skills.

Antonette's Motivated Skills

After reviewing her values, Antonette and I shifted to a discussion about the skills she enjoys using most at work each day. Here, again, are the four categories of skill motivation:

Motivated Skills – Skills you're good at and enjoy doing every day. For example, you might love conceptualizing, dealing with ambiguity, or working with numbers.

Burnout Skills – Skills you're good at but do not enjoy doing. For example, you might be proficient at working with numbers but find it tedious and draining.

Developmental Skills – Skills you would like to do more but haven't had an opportunity to develop, such as managing others. Perhaps you love managing your home budget but haven't had a chance with budget responsibility at work.

Low Priority Skills – Skills that no matter how much time you invest in them, you don't seem to significantly improve your skill level. That's OK, because you don't like to do them, either!

The following list is a combination of Antonette's motivated and developmental skills. Knowing Antonette was unfulfilled in her career as a pharmaceutical sales representative, does anything stand out about her motivated skills that might explain her career dissatisfaction?

ANTONETTE'S MOTIVATED SKILLS

Administration
n/a

Artistic & Mechanical
Entertain/Perform

Conceptual & Creative
Ambiguity (Deal with)
Conceptualize
Ideas (Generate)
Improvise
Innovate/Invent
Strategize
Synthesize
Visualize

Interpersonal
Act as Liaison
Counsel
Deal with Feelings
Perceive Intuitively
Teach/Train
Team Work

Leadership
Initiate Change
Leadership
Mentor
Motivate

Manage Process & Projects
Manage Time
Plan/Organize

Research & Analysis
Analyze
Interview for
Information
Observe
Read for Information
Research Online

Sales
Negotiate

Supervise
Decision Making
Delegate

Technical & Information
Computer Literate
Test

The following list contains Antonette's burnout and low priority skills—skills she would prefer to avoid. Knowing Antonette was unfulfilled in her career, try to identify skills she had to perform as a sales rep that contributed to her dissatisfaction.

BURNOUT AND LOW PRIORITY SKILLS

Administration
Budget
Classify
Maintain Records

Artistic & Mechanical
Portray Images
Use Mechanical Abilities

Conceptual & Creative
Design

Interpersonal
Mediate

Manage Process & Projects
Adapt to Change
Customer Service
Expedite
Implement
Make Arrangements
Monitor
Multitask

Research & Analysis
Evaluate

Sales
Sell

Supervise
Supervise

Technical & Information
Estimating
Numbers (Work with)
Proofread/Edit
Write

Antonette's Skills Insights

Antonette's highest concentration of motivated skills is in the Conceptual/Creative category, relating to mental concepts such as generating ideas, innovating, strategizing, and visualizing. If you recall, four of Antonette's strengths were in the Thinking category (Strategic, Futuristic, Learner, Input). Hence, it's unsurprising that skills related to mental concepts would be most appealing to her.

You will see common patterns and threads across your own data when you complete these assessments and exercises, which is very affirming.

Antonette's other preferred skill categories are:

- Interpersonal (Act as Liaison, Counsel, Deal with Feelings, Perceive Intuitively, Teach/Train, Teamwork)
- Research & Analysis
- Leadership

In addition to the lack of conceptual and creative skills in Antonette's role as a sales representative, another mismatch was her strong orientation to teamwork. A sales rep role involves frequent travel for client visits, which is counter to team-based work. The role of a sales representative is often independent of the team.

Notice that Selling and Customer Service are in Antonette's Low Priority and Burn Out skills. These are probably the two most important and frequently used skills of a sales representative!

Also note that Supervise is a low priority skill for her, but Leadership is not. This means Antonette will thrive most in a role where she has some level of authority for decision making and can exercise leadership through expertise and mentoring without having to manage people. Think of the power of her Strategic and Futuristic strengths to help guide and lead others forward!

At this stage, Antonette has a mismatch for the first three pillars of career satisfaction. Let's review her fourth and final pillar.

How Antonette is Wired

As introduced earlier, Holland Occupational Themes is based on six personality types. To recap, they are Realistic, Investigative, Artistic, Social, Enterprising, and Conventional.

After assessing Antonette's career interests, I looked at her top two highest ranking career interest codes. Her highest was Investigative, followed by Social, as shown here:

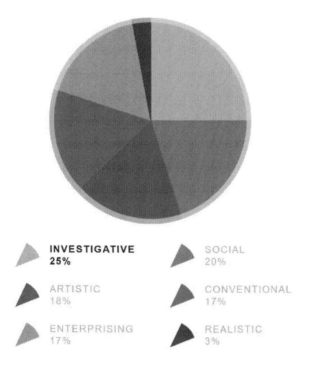

INVESTIGATIVE
25%

SOCIAL
20%

ARTISTIC
18%

CONVENTIONAL
17%

ENTERPRISING
17%

REALISTIC
3%

We know that Antonette has four Thinking strengths in her StrengthsFinder results. Again, we see consistency across her assessments, as Thinking strengths correlate with the Investigative career type (The Thinkers). Teamwork is also important to Antonette, which is consistent with a Social career interest orientation.

Antonette's Career Interest Type: The Practitioner (Investigative/Social)

CareerCode: Know Your Code, Find Your Fit by Lowe and Lungrin provides a nice characterization of the I/S career type:

I/Ss are often caring, diagnostic, cautious, curious, analytical, overextended (take on more than they have time for when people need their help), independent, intellectual, objective, and introverted.

Healthcare is a typical field for those with an I/S code because much of the work revolves around helping others, thinking objectively, and solving challenging problems. An I/S will likely feel fulfilled in healthcare jobs that involve contact with patients or staff and makes a difference for others.

Interestingly, when reviewing her career interest code, Antonette shared she had once considered becoming a medical doctor but didn't end up pursuing the profession. When working with clients, I will ask them about careers they've considered but didn't pursue. Often their early instincts about their interests are consistent with what we uncover in coaching.

The need for I/S individuals in the workplace is great because most I/S careers are in healthcare, which requires a scientific approach with a social orientation. These jobs will stay in high demand, especially with an aging population. Jobs in certain medical and health specialties are far more plentiful in larger metropolitan areas, while more general I/S jobs are widely available everywhere.

During our final session, I asked Antonette to strike out anything she disagreed with in the I/S profile above. We also discussed career ideas for next steps, and I helped her evaluate them against her YouMap® information.

After much reflection on what she had learned about herself, she decided to transition from sales into teaching and training. This career choice uses a combination of her thinking preference and her social orientation to help others. She began teaching business classes in the evening at a local college with the intention of seeking a full-time training role during the day.

If you'd like a deeper explanation of your career type, consider picking up a copy of CareerCode: Know Your Code, Find Your Fit.

In the next section, I'll introduce tools and methods you can use to investigate and evaluate career options.

Blaze Your Path

"There are plenty of difficult obstacles in your path.
Don't allow yourself to become one of them."
– Ralph Marston, Author

Information without application can leave you feeling stuck. Therefore, the next important step is to tackle the question, "Now what?" Blazing a new path can be difficult, but nothing that's worth anything is ever easy. Jim Rohn said, "If you really want to do something, you'll find a way. If you don't, you'll find an excuse."

"Blaze Your Path" will help you figure out what to do with all the information we unearthed in the first section of the book—resulting in your YouMap®—and apply it practically to gain clarity and focus.

To make the most of this section, you should complete at least a rough first draft of your YouMap®. In "Find Yourself," you received a lot of information about what makes you who you are. If you haven't completed that first step, consider doing so before moving forward because you will use your YouMap® to complete tasks in this section.

After you've completed the "Find Yourself" section, you might think one of the following statements sounds like you:

1. "I'm in the right kind of role. I'm just not performing the role in the right workplace environment or industry, or for the right manager." This usually happens when the biggest cause of role misfit relates to your values and to some extent your skills, depending on how your manager or organization established your job description.
2. "The discovery process confirmed the career path I'm considering appears to fit well with my YouMap® insights."
3. "I'm on an entirely wrong career path, and a career change is in

order."

4."It's become clear I no longer want to be an employee of someone else."

If number one or two sounds like you, you can read this section or skip to the next section. However, I recommend you check out the tips in "Job Boards and Job Descriptions" and "Informational Interviews" before you skip ahead to "Show the World!", where practical strategies will be shared to communicate your value proposition in networking conversations, cover letters, resumes, LinkedIn profiles, and interviews.

If number three sounds like you, you should work through this section to gain clarity and direction.

If you relate to number four, you will find additional information in "Show the World!". I also recommend taking an entrepreneurial strengths assessment called "Builder Profile 10," created by the Gallup organization. After years of research, Gallup has identified ten innate talents entrepreneurs share. At the time of this writing the profile is US$19.99.

The ten entrepreneurial talents are: Determination, Confidence, Knowledge, Relationship, Disruptor, Risk, Independence, Delegator, Selling, and Profitability. These ten talents combine to create distinct entrepreneurial styles. This can help you assess your entrepreneurial strengths and where you might need support.

You can take the Builder 10 Profile here: tinyurl.com/ya5lvyd6

Next, I'd like to introduce you to some resources and techniques I use with my own clients to help them make career decisions. The first is O*NET.

Introduction to O*NET

The O*NET (Occupational Information Network) Program is the United States' primary source of occupational information.

Central to this program is the O*NET database, containing hundreds of standardized and occupation-specific descriptors on approximately 1,000 occupations throughout the US. The database is accessible at no cost and is continually updated from input by a broad range of workers in each occupation.

O*NET information is used by millions of individuals annually, including those taking advantage of O*NET Online and My Next Move, which are two features of O*NET I will cover below. O*NET is developed under the sponsorship of the US Department of Labor/Employment and Training Administration (USDOL/ETA).

You can access O*NET online at www.onetonline.org

One of my favorite features of the O*NET online site is the Career Interest Profiler.

Career Interest Profiler

This interest profiler is built on the personality-based Holland Occupational Themes I introduced in Discover How You're Wired in the "Find Yourself" section.

The profiler provides three ways to approach career discovery.

Search Option 1: "I want to be a…"

This feature allows you to describe your ideal career using key word searches. For example, I entered "Help people heal" into the search box, and the following list of occupations returned in the search results:

• Home Health Aides
• Community Health Workers
• Occupational Health & Safety Technicians
• Health Educators
• Mental Health Counselors
• Occupational Health & Safety Specialists

- Sociologists
- Occupational Therapists
- Veterinary Assistants & Laboratory Animal Caretakers
- Medical & Health Services Managers

Search Option 2: "I'll know it when I see it…"

This search option allows you to discover careers by industry, such as Education, Health & Counseling, Media & Communication, Management, Manufacturing, and others.

Once an industry selection is made, a list of occupations in your selected industry is returned and includes additional helpful information, such as the occupation's projected growth, which is referred to as a Bright Outlook field in O*NET.

Search Option 3: "I'm not really sure…"

This option invites you to take the Career Interest Profiler. After you complete the short profiler assessment, the site returns your Holland Occupational Code results. I have included my results here as an example.

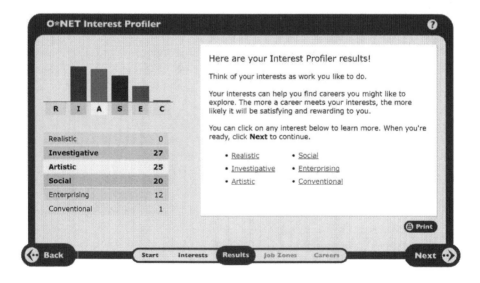

In my example, my primary career interest is Investigative (27%), followed by Artistic (25%), with my top three types shown above in bold (Investigative, Artistic, Social – Thinker/Creator/Helper). The Investigative/Artistic combination is known as The Scholar and suggests I should picture myself as a sociologist.

I've never wanted to be a sociologist (and I still don't), even though the field intrigues me. If you recall, I suggested treating the career recommendations as instructive rather than firm suggestions.

Let's review the description of The Scholar: highly observant, deep thinkers, intuitive, insightful, complex, researcher, introverted, intellectual, independent, opinionated.

I agree those descriptors sound like me (though I'm not an introvert). Interestingly, if I flip my first two codes to Artistic/Investigative, The Idealist, the career suggestion is an author!

After my career code results appeared, I clicked the "Next" button in the bottom right corner to move to the next step of focusing my occupation search by Interest and Job Zone. Job Zones group occupations into one of five categories based on level of education, experience, and training necessary to perform the job, as follows:

Job Zone 1 – Requires little to no preparation and could be performed without formal education and with little training.

Job Zone 2 – Requires some preparation and might require a training program for a pre-determined number of weeks or prior experience.

Job Zone 3 – Requires moderate preparation and could require an Associate's or Bachelor's degree plus three years of experience.

Job Zone 4 – Requires considerable preparation and could require post-graduate education such as a Master's degree and five to seven years of work experience.

Job Zone 5 – Requires extensive preparation and could require a Doctoral degree and Post-Doctoral training or a Master's degree with an additional license.

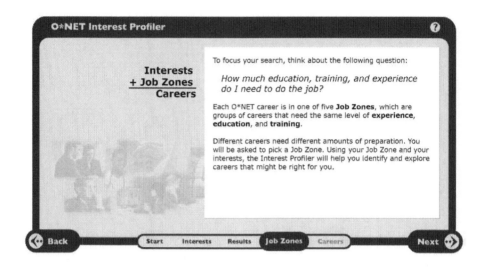

I selected Job Zone 4 to retrieve a list of occupations according to my interest and desired job zone, which is displayed below. I'm not entirely surprised to see Creative Writers as an occupational match (although I prefer to write prescriptive nonfiction), nor was I surprised to see a Career/Technical Education Teacher match in my list. Though, I certainly wouldn't be interested in performing a career education role at the middle school level because I know I work best with individuals who are in high school and older. Think of the career recommendations as a starting point for your research.

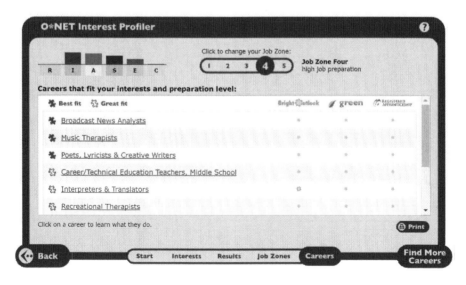

If you're an active member of the military, or a veteran (Thank you for your service!), there's also a Career Interest Profiler available just for you. It enables you to select the military branch in which you serve(d) and your MOS classification. The Career Interest Profiler will return private sector job recommendations that are most similar to your MOS. The roles are not necessarily in specific tasks but in the underlying career interests associated with your classification.

For example, if you were in the Army with MOS classification 13F, Joint Fire Support Specialist - Enlisted, the Career Interest Profiler would return occupations that might appeal to similar personalities interested in data, detail, regular routine, and additional matching factors.

If you've had a long military career, consider finding a mentor who has had similar experiences and has also successfully transitioned to a career in the private sector. Mentorship by someone who has traveled the road you are pursuing is going to be much more beneficial than using the Career Interest Profiler alone.

You can take the Career Interest Profiler at the My Next Move website using the following links:

Military Veteran Career Interest Profile
 www.mynextmove.org/vets/
Standard Career Interest Profiler
www.mynextmove.org/explore/ip
Spanish Language Career Interest Profiler
www.miproximopaso.org/

O*NET Occupational Database

After you have your career interest results, you'll notice each of the possible occupation matches are hyperlinked. This is where the Career Interest Profiler integrates with the O*NET Occupational Database. You can click on any occupation title and review a wealth of information about that occupation contained in the O*NET Occupational Database.

The images below capture the information displayed when I clicked the

Career/Technical Education Teachers, Middle School occupation title in my Career Interest Profiler results.

You'll notice a description of the occupation includes the core responsibilities. In addition, it provides the knowledge, skills, and abilities related to the role, personality characteristics associated with the occupation, technology skills needed, required education, and the projected outlook for the occupation (growing, steady, or shrinking field).

Additional links encourage you to explore a sample of additional, related occupations if the occupation you're researching doesn't seem quite right for you.

Take a moment to review the images below to familiarize yourself with the information the O*NET Occupational Database provides. Make note of the "Also called" section at the top left beneath the job title. This is a useful source of information to search opportunities on job boards by job title.

Career/Technical Education Teachers, Middle School

Also called: Family and Consumer Sciences Teacher (FACS Teacher), Teacher, Technology Education Teacher, Technology Teacher

What they do:
Teach occupational, career and technical, or vocational subjects in public or private schools at the middle, intermediate, or junior high level, which falls between elementary and senior high school as defined by applicable laws and regulations.

On the job, you would:
- Instruct and monitor students in the use and care of equipment and materials to prevent injuries and damage.
- Establish and enforce rules for behavior and procedures for maintaining order among students.
- Adapt teaching methods and instructional materials to meet students' varying needs and interests.

KNOWLEDGE

Education and Training
- teaching and course design

Arts and Humanities
- English language

Engineering and Technology
- computers and electronics

Math and Science
- psychology

SKILLS

Basic Skills
- reading work related information
- talking to others

Social
- teaching people how to do something
- understanding people's reactions

Problem Solving
- noticing a problem and figuring out the best way to solve it

ABILITIES

Verbal
- communicate by speaking
- listen and understand what people say

Ideas and Logic
- notice when problems happen
- use rules to solve problems

Attention
- do two or more things at the same time
- pay attention to something without being distracted

PERSONALITY

People interested in this work like activities that include helping people, teaching, and talking.

They do well at jobs that need:
- Dependability
- Integrity
- Self Control
- Stress Tolerance
- Adaptability/Flexibility
- Cooperation

TECHNOLOGY

You might use software like this on the job:

Computer based training software
- Blackboard Learn
- Desire2Learn

Word processing software
- Collaborative editing software
- Google Docs

Electronic mail software
- Email software
- Microsoft Outlook

EDUCATION

bachelor's degree or master's degree usually needed

Get started on your career:
- Find Training
- Find Certifications
- Find Licenses

JOB OUTLOOK

Average — New job opportunities are likely in the future.

SALARY: **$57,560**

$38,670 — $87,980
- Check out my state
- Local Salary Info
- Find Jobs

EXPLORE MORE
- Mental Health & Substance Abuse Social Workers
- Nursing Instructors & Teachers, Postsecondary
- Recreational Therapists
- Special Education Teachers, Secondary School
- Substance Abuse & Behavioral Disorder Counselors

You might like a career in one of these industries:
- Education

You can also access the O*NET Occupational Database directly without completing the Career Interest Profiler by going to www.onetonline.org and entering occupation titles into the search box in the upper right corner of the site. Notice also, the "Explore More" section lists some additional occupations and industries you might be interested in.

> **Tip**: To obtain a complete list of suggested occupation matches based on your interest code, go to www.onetonline.org. Click "Advanced Search" from the main menu, then select "Interests" from the Advanced Search submenu. The six Holland codes will display as hyperlinks. Click your primary interest code, and then select your secondary interest code from the drop down and click "Go." An expanded list of career options will display for you to research.

Use the space below to capture occupations of interest and any details about those occupations you want to note. List requirements needed to pursue the occupation such as education, certification, or experience. Next, rank desirability of pursuing the option (low, medium, high) and feasibility (low, medium, high). Feasibility is usually related to resources, such as time and money. Select the most feasible, then most desirable, option. Download my Career Decision-

Making Tool at MyYouMap.com.

_____

_____

_____

_____

_____

_____

_____

_____

_____

_____

_____

If your most feasible and desirable career option requires additional credentials, training, education, or licensure, O*NET can help you obtain more information regarding education, too. When you search occupations using the quick search from the www.onetonline.org home page, the detailed results for each occupation include an "Education" section near the bottom of the occupation summary report.

The following example is for a mechanical engineer. Notice the survey respondents working in this job title indicate their current level of education. You can see 85% of mechanical engineers have a Bachelor's degree. You can click on Find Training, Find Certifications, Find Licenses, and Find Apprenticeships to discover education and training opportunities for your desired occupation by geographic area.

Another helpful resource to identify education requirements for various occupations is Study.com. Or you can go directly to study.com/directory/category/index.html to search degrees by subject (engineering, business, architecture, psychology, etc.).

Job Boards and Job Descriptions

Once you've researched occupations of interest using the O*NET Occupational Database, you're ready to begin using job boards to search job descriptions to discover what employers are looking for. This also helps you confirm job descriptions align with your research on O*NET and your current expectations.

Job boards I prefer to use to search postings are Indeed.com, Glassdoor.com, LinkedIn.com, CareerBuilder.com, and Crossroadscareer.org.

> **Tip**: Online searching should comprise the smallest percentage of your job search time, no more than 10-25%. The purpose of job board searching is to identify opportunities you can use as a basis to network with other people. Your goal is to identify companies hiring for positions you're well suited for and then use both online and in-person networking to reveal people you know who can make an introduction into the organization.

Not sure what job titles to search? I recommend two strategies:

1. Create keyword searches from your YouMap® by combining a strength or description from My Strengths and How I'm Wired sections, plus a skill from the My Skills section.

For example, if you're strategic and you like project management, you can search "strategic project management" on the job board. If you have your Six Sigma Green Belt or PMP certification enter that into the job board search, as job descriptions are fully searchable, and you might not know what jobs require a credential you hold.

You can also search a functional skill plus the target industry, such as "Program Management Healthcare." Get creative with your searches!

2. Use the O*NET Occupational Database by navigating in a browser to www.onetonline.org. Next, enter the occupation in the Occupation Quick Search box in the upper right corner.

For example, if you're looking for an IT project manager role, enter that into the Occupation Quick Search. In the returned results, click the hyperlinked Information Technology Project Manager occupation.

Near the top of the Summary Report you will see a section titled, "Sample of Reported Job Titles." The Bureau of Labor Statistics reports on job titles based on the current labor market.

For the IT project manager example, you will see in the Sample of Reported Job Titles section the following job titles listed for individuals employed in the information technology project management field. You can paste these titles into the search feature of job boards.

IT Manager, IT Project Manager, Manager of IT, Program Manager, Project Manager, Project Manager/Team Coach, Senior Lead Project Manager, Senior Project Leader/Team Lead, Technical Project Lead (Project Manager), Transition Program Manager.

Remember when I asked you to complete the highlighting exercise of your deal makers and deal breakers at the end of "Find Yourself?" Your YouMap® will prove useful here, as you can compare a job description against the deal makers and deal breakers you highlighted in your profile.

As you research job descriptions, compare those descriptions to your highlighted checklist of deal makers and deal breakers in your YouMap®. How does the job description compare to the skills you have highlighted? Do you see more burnout skills highlighted than motivating skills? Does it appear you will use your strengths in this role? If the job description doesn't seem to resonate with the "How I'm Wired" section, proceed with caution. Make a note of any concerns you have and bring those to the next step in the process: testing the waters!

Entering a new career can create feelings of uncertainty and overwhelm for many. You might be wondering if you'll be as good in another role as you are in current or previous roles. If you're a recent graduate who hasn't entered the workforce, you might be even more unsure. Following are several suggestions to test the waters before taking the leap into a new career.

Informational Interviews

Informational interviews involve informal conversations with someone who works, or has worked, in an area that appeals to you. You can leverage your entire network to see whom you might be interested in speaking with regarding the opportunities you're considering.

Some readers might be skeptical, thinking they don't have a very large network of people to ask, but your network is probably larger than you think. Here are just a few networking sources you might not have considered:

- People with whom you volunteer, engage in hobbies, play sports, or go to church
- Alumni or professors from your academic institution
- Past or present coworkers
- Friends and family
- Professional associations or clubs where you are a member
- Mentors or business contacts
- Former or current employees of companies you're targeting
- Vendors or customers you know
- Recruiters

Your YouMap® will be an invaluable resource for informational interviews because it gives the person you're speaking with a quick and distilled snapshot of your assets. At a glance, he or she will be able to see the daily work activities you enjoy and the value you bring as described in the My Unique Contribution statement. This enables your networking contact to generate ideas about roles he or she is aware of that align strongly with your profile. In "Show the World!", I'll introduce you to creating a networking conversation and a networking sheet to use in these conversations.

When I was in college studying neuroscience in the Department of

Psychology, my mother arranged an informational interview between me and a neurologist she knew professionally. After our meeting I knew neuroscience wasn't right for me. I was thankful for the informational interview!

One final note for career changers thinking about what's next. Remember that for most people a career path is often not linear. In this video, "Seven Lessons About Career Change," INSEAD Professor Herminia Ibarra and six people who have successfully transitioned careers are interviewed and share some useful lessons about career change.

youtu.be/NKwYTmHExWQ

Volunteer Work

If your potential next career step is one where you have little or no direct experience, a good way to gain experience and test if you like the job is through volunteer work. I performed career coaching as a volunteer and coached hundreds of people by the time I decided on career coaching as my main profession. Shifting from volunteer to paid coaching was a smooth transition because I already had word-of-mouth referrals from pro bono clients. I also created a formal coaching process to guarantee consistent methods to coach each person with excellence.

A former coworker tried her hand in editing and copywriting for a local nonprofit by volunteering to produce their monthly newsletter.

Volunteer organizations offer opportunities to dabble in event planning, photography, cooking, life coaching, graphic design, audio/visual production, financial planning, project management, program administration, teaching, training, public speaking, fundraising, grant writing, marketing, elementary education, sales, and much more. Volunteer work can also be a valuable way to gain management experience if you're an individual contributor considering a move to management.

Years ago, I volunteered as an Awana Commander at my church. I launched the program from scratch and recruited volunteers. I was responsible for leading and training about twenty-one volunteers. While leading the team was unpaid experience, I contend that leading people who aren't paid to be there can be far more challenging than managing people who are paid to show up!

Volunteer work isn't suitable for everyone. You might be a single mom or dad with limited child care options or working two jobs to make ends meet. If taking on volunteer work would place undue stress on you or your family, you can disregard this suggestion.

The Side Hustle

While starting a business on the side isn't for everyone and won't work universally with all occupations (like brain surgeons), a side hustle can be another way to test the waters.

Here are some things to consider when starting a side hustle:

- First, define your model customer and then the services you might provide your customer.
- Save six months of expenses to enable you to quit your job. Make radical lifestyle changes if needed.
- Figure out your services, scheduling, proposal and invoice process before other aspects of the business. Don't try to build everything at once; concentrate on your operational needs. Perhaps a website can come later, for example.
- Seek a few unpaid jobs or, better yet, barter and trade services to refine your process and ask those people to write an online testimonial.
- Interact on social media related to your product or service to generate interest.
- Emphasize being a giver not a taker. Constantly pushing your wares will turn people off.
- Develop customer-centric messaging on the pain you solve for your customer. Explain why and what, not how.
- Go to networking events and share your why.

I asked side hustle advice from some other business owners in my network, and here is what they added:

- Laura advises to remember to set aside payments for taxes because

you're responsible for paying them.
- Michael says to leap! When you're sitting still, nothing happens.
- Crystal suggests having business cards with dedicated business contact details to lend credibility.
- Joseph suggests always keep learning and refining your process. He does not agree that you should ever work for free as it could lessen your perceived value.
- Raina says to network effectively by engaging with the right people.

What if you would love to work for yourself, but you have no idea what you would do?

Sam Horn, CEO of The Intrigue Agency and TEDx speaker, gave me permission to share her story explaining how she created the career she loves and her advice on how you can too. The following was originally written by Sam as a blog post.

"Finding your passion isn't just about careers and money. It's about finding your authentic self. The one you've buried beneath other people's needs."
– Kristen Hannah

One of the keys to doing work you love is to stop thinking you will find it—as if it exists out there intact—and all you have to do is look long and hard enough, and EUREKA, there it will be, hiding behind a tree.

Work we love more often emerges from doing something we're good at, something that matters to us, something that when we do it we feels authentic, like we're doing what we were born to do. It is a result of acting on what calls us and creating a career path that is congruent with what we care about.

You may be thinking, "Sounds good in theory, but HOW do I do this in practice?"

Well, here's how I created my career as a professional speaker/author/consultant. I didn't even know this profession existed when I was growing up. There was no major or degree in this at college. No newspaper ads with job announcements hiring for this type of work. No map to follow. No directions.

The work I'm doing is the result of intuitive yet strategic steps I took along the way that honored what I call the Four I's of our Career Compass. When I had career decisions to make and didn't know what to do, I checked in with my Instincts, Interests, Integrity, Initiative.

Invariably, the Four I's pointed me in the right direction and provided my next step. Honoring my Career Compass has yielded a deep and truly satisfying success that feels right in my heart.

It started back when I needed to make my first major career decision: What was I going to major in at college? Thanks to my dad giving me an inspiring quote by W. H. Murray and encouraging me to be bold on behalf of what felt right, I had the prescience to honor my four I's.

Instincts: My instincts were telling me to follow my heart and study Recreation Administration instead of following other people's advice to take the traditional option of being a doctor or lawyer.

Interests: I loved playing, coaching, and organizing sports and recreational activities so studying Recreation Administration was in alignment with my interests.

Integrity: I wanted a career that added value. Money was not my primary motivator. Doing something that mattered and that would make a positive difference for people was my priority.

Initiative: I didn't wait for job opportunities to come my way. I actively sought out and pitched myself into professional opportunities that were in alignment with my other three I's.

A college student named Mark said, "Okay, I get the Four I's, but how did that lead to your current career?"

"Years ago, I was reading The Washington Post and noticed the word concentration was used six times in the sports section. Tennis player Chrissie Evert said her ability to stay focused despite the planes flying overhead was why she'd been able to win the US Open. A golfer who missed a putt on a sudden death playoff hole said he'd lost his concentration because of the clicking cameras of nearby photographers.

"I was intrigued. (I now know that when we're intrigued, opportunity is knocking on our heart.)

"I thought, 'We all wish we could concentrate better, but no one ever teaches us how. Concentration is the key to success in just about everything—business, relationships, sports and life—but I've never seen any books or heard any speakers on this subject. And it matters.'

"This topic interested me. I felt it was an important personal and professional skill that would benefit people, so it was in alignment with my integrity. And my instincts were telling me there was a commercial need for this and people would pay to be taught how to do it better.

"I decided to initiate a deep dive into the topic of concentration with the goal of offering public workshops on it. Instead of reading other people's work, I created a ten question W quiz to kick-start anecdotal research. I interviewed 'everyday people' to glean their insights and examples. My W questions included:

1. What does concentration mean to you? How would you define it?
2. Who modeled or taught concentration to you? Who is a shining example of someone who does it well? Was it a coach, teacher, parent, surgeon, musician? Why are they good at it?
3. Who is an example of someone who does NOT concentrate well? Why are they not good at it? Are they constantly distracted, preoccupied, all over the map? What?
4. When is a time you concentrated well? Were you skiing a black diamond slope, reading, with someone you love, working to a deadline? What facilitated that state of focus and flow?
5. When is a time you didn't concentrate well? What blocked or prevented your focus or flow? Was it noisy? Were you stressed, distracted, preoccupied, worrying about something? Explain.
6. Why is concentration important? Why is it to our benefit to be able to do it well?
7. Why don't we do it well then? Is it because no one teaches us? Because we have too many things competing for our attention?

Because we don't discipline our mind? What?

8. Where do you concentrate best? Do you have a special place where you can attain that exquisite state of full focus and flow? Describe it.

9. What is your best advice about how to concentrate? What can I cover in my workshops that you would like to learn, that would be useful to know?

10. Who else do you think I should interview about this topic? Who would be a good resource who has valuable advice on how to get good at this?

"Based on the fascinating answers to this W quiz (and my own experience as an athlete), I developed a step-by-step approach on how to concentrate—no matter what—and offered it for Washington, D.C.'s Open University. At the end of that first program, several participants came up and said, 'We need this in our organization. Will you teach our employees (or association members) how to do this?'

"That one workshop launched a rewarding career that has taken me around the world and given me opportunities to work with the US Embassy in London, Capital One, INC 500, Boeing, National Geographic, and Intel. It even resulted in a book that's been featured on NPR, taught at NASA, and was endorsed by Stephen Covey and Dr. Ed Hallowell (a leading expert on A.D.D.)."

Mark said, "Okay, I got how this kick-started your career. By why the quiz?"

"The goal is to develop your own intellectual capital. It's important to bring your own original experience, one-of-a-kind expertise and epiphanies to the table instead of just adopting other experts' best-practices into your work.

"'Street interviews' with everyday people helps you create a unique body of work. Interview everyone. Taxi drivers. Waiters and waitresses. Friends and family members. Educators, attorneys, athletes, artists, entrepreneurs. People love being asked for their stories and advice, and it steeps you in your subject and guarantees you are addressing current needs and challenges and offering real-life insights that work.

"Like I did with the topic of Concentration, you can create a quality course, service, and business wrapped around what you know that other people want to know. Creating a replicable, step-by-step methodology provides a shortcut to people's success so they don't have to start from scratch and figure it out [on] their own.

"People will gladly pay for your creation because you're saving them time, money and hassle by expediting their path to get better at something they care about. If you do this, you'll never have to 'work' another day in your life because you'll be earning a good living doing work you love with people you enjoy and respect. And isn't that what we all want?

"Want an example? Woody and Eleanor Ruff were two retired teachers who wanted to write a book about everything their students wished their parents knew. We came up with a perfect title, Long Days, Short Years. Eleanor called to say they'd been asked to speak on a cruise but were going to turn it down because they were on a tight deadline and were afraid they wouldn't finish their manuscript on time.

"I said, 'Don't cancel the cruise! There will be a thousand parents and grandparents on board. What a perfect opportunity to interview people from all walks of life from all parts of the globe. Just take your version of the W quiz and connect with people at meals and while walking around the ship.'

"They got back in touch to say, 'We were the hit of the ship! Everyone wanted to share their advice about what they had done they were happy about and what they wish they had done differently.'

"So, what do you know that other people would like to know? What is something you're good at people would like to get good at?

"Maybe people tell you how much they love your iPhone photos and ask, 'How do you take such great pictures?' Maybe people admire how well-trained your dogs are and say, 'I wish my dogs behaved like that.'

"The first step to creating a meaningful career where you get paid to do work you love is to leverage your talents and skills into a business where people pay you to do that FOR them or to teach that TO them."

Want more ideas? Check out Sam Horn's book, IDEApreneur: Monetize Your Mind at tinyurl.com/ycshmcnh.

Stretch Projects

If you're currently employed, it might be possible to gain exposure to potential new roles through special projects. As part of your goal planning for the upcoming year, you can approach your manager with stretch project ideas, perhaps collaborating with someone in a role you're interested in moving into.

When I was working as a Learning & Development leader, one of my direct reports, Charlene, was really interested in creating learning content and graphic design. As part of her stretch goals, I had her collaborate with our Instructional Design Manager, Kimberly.

Charlene learned to use instructional design tools and was able to tap into her creative nature to generate graphics for training modules. She later went on to complete a User Experience (UX) Design program and has now transitioned from a training coordinator to a UX designer.

Job Shadowing

Job shadowing pairs you with a person experienced in a specific role to give you a glimpse into a day in the life of someone working in your target role. This person can show you the ropes and answer questions to help you determine the suitability of a role and the path they took to get there.

Remember to share your YouMap® with the person you shadow so they can weigh in on your role fit. If you're currently employed, speak to your manager, mentor, or coworkers about job shadowing opportunities.

Mentoring

A mentoring relationship is one of the best ways to advance, or even transition, your career. Your mentor should be someone who has worked in the role you're seeking because they know what it takes to do the job and can offer useful development advice.

When I was an operations manager, I asked the vice president over Learning & Development to be my mentor. When a position opened on the team, I applied. Because my mentor had experience with me, she knew I was ambitious, strategic, and had strong interpersonal skills.

I ended up getting the job, which I doubt would have happened if not for the exposure from the mentoring relationship.

Mentors are advisors. They suggest direction, identify obstacles, and assist you in overcoming those obstacles. Mentors are an ally. They provide candid, forthright opinions to increase your self-awareness. Mentors serve as brokers by assisting you with establishing and increasing your network contacts. Mentors are also catalysts. They promote understanding of organizational culture and clarify employer expectations. Finally, they are communicators who facilitate discussion, interaction, and the exchange of information.

Your role as a mentee is to:

- Fully engage in the relationship
- Be open to constructive feedback
- Set meetings and agendas
- Show up on time and prepared for scheduled meetings
- Follow up on action items
- Identify and track goals
- Align key learnings from the mentor with your own situation

Emily, one of my former direct reports, was interested in transitioning from training to project management. I introduced her to my friend, Vidya, who was a manager in the Project Management Office. Vidya began mentoring Emily, resulting in an opportunity for promotion that might not have happened without Vidya's sponsorship of her.

Any serious career management plan should enlist the help of a mentor.

Tip: To choose a mentor, identify someone who is or has been in a role you're considering. Share your career goals and the time commitment you're asking them to make. Maybe it's one hour per month. If they can't mentor you at this time, explain why you chose him or her and ask if they would suggest another mentor and perhaps make the introduction. Leverage their network so you're not starting at zero again.

Internships

Internships are a great way to get in the trenches and experience a role firsthand. You can use LinkedIn.com and Glassdoor.com to find internships as well as websites created for that purpose, such as Internships.com and WayUp.com.

A couple of years ago I led a career workshop at a high school and asked participants to raise their hand if they had experienced an internship. One of the students shared what he learned from his internship: "That I never want to work in an office."

Some internships are paid; some are not. Not everyone can afford to work in an unpaid internship. Other options to research are the Peace Corps in the US, CUSO in Canada, and European Solidarity Corps in the EU. You can also search "Paid Internships" in your area.

Learning what you don't want is valuable information.

Work Attribute Preferences

Speaking of learning what you don't want, not only do internal drivers lead to career satisfaction, but external drivers, as well. The YouMap® defines internal drivers of career fulfillment. However, it's also important to consider environmental variables. Start with your internal drivers of career motivation, and then narrow down your choices by ruling out options that do not have desirable environmental attributes.

The American College Testing (ACT) Program has identified twenty-five common attributes of work associated with personal job satisfaction. The assumption is if the attributes of a job match one's personal preferences, then one is more likely to be satisfied in that job, all other things being equal. Below you will find the twenty-five Work Attribute Preferences (WAPs) listed alphabetically with their definitions. Sample jobs associated with each attribute are shown in parentheses.

1. **Authority**: Similar to management, but toward nonemployees, as in a traffic cop job—telling people what to do or what not to do (lawyer, consultant)
2. **Certification**: Careers certifying competence by a degree, license, etc. (doctor, actuary, Realtor)
3. **Creating Order**: Using rules to arrange things (quality inspector, administrator)
4. **Easy Re-entry**: Easy to move or quit and come back, as after maternity leave (sales, mechanic)
5. **Financial Challenge**: Advising others so that much could be gained or lost (investment/financial planner)
6. **40-hour week**: Work that entails no overtime, taking work home, on-call status, etc. (postal clerk)

7. **High Income**: To be in the top 25% of money earners (NFL quarterback, executive)

8. **Immediate Response**: Working/performing around others where immediate feedback is the norm, such as applause, laughs, boos, cheers, attaboys, handshakes, etc. (comedian, flight attendant)

9. **Influencing Others**: Convincing without authority (sales, counseling, health care, social work)

10. **Making or Fixing Things**: Working with your hands or tools on electro-mechanical objects (mechanic)

11. **Management: Planning**, directing, and evaluating the work of others (manager, supervisor)

12. **New Ideas**: Creating new ways to do things—trying new combinations of ideas (advertising, consultant)

13. **Non-Standard Hours**: Preferring work that is seasonal, temporary, part-time, shifts, etc. (consultant)

14. **Occasional Travel**: Out of town travel about once each quarter (small business owner)

15. **Physical Activity**: Work that results in a significant amount of exercise—walking, lifting, sporting (construction, firefighter, baggage handler)

16. **Precision**: Work that is done according to exact standards or procedures (assembler, fabricator)

17. **Problem Solving**: Spending time figuring out how to do things, to get things done, to fix things (consultant)

18. **Project Work**: Tasks lasting one week or longer (project manager, engineer, architect)

19. **Public Contact**: Work in which you can talk and be seen by non-coworkers (customer service, sales)

20. **Routine Travel**: Getting out of the office/town once each week or more (many sales positions, consultant)

21. **Short Training Time**: Requires less than six months' training after high school (construction work, receptionist, delivery driver)

22. **Working in an Office**: Working most of the time inside, in an office (accountant, writer, banker)

23. **Working In/Out**: Working partially inside and partially outside

(material handler, elementary school teacher, coach)

24. **Working Outside**: Working outdoors in the weather, good or bad (cowboy letter carrier, door-to-door sales)

25. **Working Separately**: Requiring little talking or other contact with coworkers (bookkeeper)

To evaluate a role's fit against your desired workplace attributes, create three simple columns like the table shown below.

List the twenty-five work attributes in the first column.

The second column is where you capture if the attributes appeal to you (Y/N/?).

In the second column, after reading each definition, indicate "Y" for yes (Yes indicates you like the attribute.), "N" for no (No indicates you don't like the attribute.), and "?" (A question mark indicates you're unsure or neutral about the attribute.). For example, if you don't want to work with the public put "N" in the second column next to Public Contact.

The third column indicates if the attribute is present in the role.

In the third column, indicate "Y", "N", or "?" for opportunities you're considering based on the knowledge you've gained by working through the "Blaze Your Path" section and researching the role.

Work Attributes	Y/N/?	Role
40-hour week	N	Y
Authority	Y	Y
Certification	N	Y
Creating Order	N	N
Easy Re-Entry	?	?
Financial Challenge	N	Y
High Income	Y	Y
Immediate Response	N	N
Influencing Others	Y	?
Making or Fixing Things	N	N
Management	Y	N
New Ideas	Y	Y
Non-Standard Hours	Y	N
Occasional Travel	Y	N
Physical Activity	N	N
Precision	N	N
Problem Solving	N	Y
Project Work	Y	N
Public Contact	N	Y
Routine Travel	N	N
Short Training Time	N	Y
Working in an Office	Y	Y
Working In/Out	N	N
Working Outside	N	N
Working Separately	Y	N

Add additional columns if you're evaluating multiple opportunities and rename the "Role" heading with actual job titles.

Finally, assess the gap between your desired attributes and the actual attributes of the role. For example, how many attribute matches are there? How many mismatched attributes?

After doing your research, speaking to others, evaluating the workplace attributes, and testing the waters, you should have a better idea of your next step. If the occupation you were considering doesn't turn out to capture your interest, you can review your YouMap® again and discuss it with trusted advisors or mentors who can make suggestions based on your information.

If you end up identifying a new direction, you can begin the process again with the research phase and then work through the recommendations in "Blaze Your Path" with your new target. Try not to be frustrated with the process. Life isn't linear, and a big component of career exploration is experiential discovery. If you've selected your next career move, let's move on to the next step: "Show the World!".

My brother, who is also an author, wrote this wonderful piece about the nonlinear nature of life, which I included as the foreword in my first book, Follow Your Star: Career Lessons I Learned from Mom. I include it again here because the lesson is priceless.

What I've Learned by Looking at Trees
by Wayne K. Spear

HAVE YOU EVER WONDERED, as I did recently, what determines the seemingly random pattern of tree branches?

A case of "every which way," it appears. One branch projects confidently toward the sky—another launches tentatively in one direction, suddenly adopting a new trajectory.

A life is the same.

I know this, because I can see my own life in these branches. That little ragged outgrowth that goes nowhere? That's a girl I dated in high school. The long, straight branch which stops suddenly? An office job I once had. The fat branch with many small offshoots? My writing career. The trunk? That represents my upbringing: the formative experiences which established my values, outlook, and dreams.

To this day, my trunk is nourishing the new branches which sprout in my life.

I noticed that there are a lot of dead ends on a tree: but look at those branches, and you'll see many outgrowths. Again, I think of the times I've come to the end of a path. Maybe it was a goal I didn't reach, or a job I didn't get.

When you're standing at the end of a path you thought and hoped would go farther, you only see losses and failures—the job you didn't get, the money you won't make, and the things you won't be able to do and have because you won't get that pay check.

Looking back, you can see that those endings are in fact launching points, like new shoots from a branch. My first business, which I created in high school, was the result of having the doors to gainful employment shut in my face. Within a month, I had more business than I could manage. I made more money and was far happier than I would have been in a job, but I felt depressed and defeated all the same when my plan to be hired by someone else didn't work out.

What I learned by looking at trees is that you can reverse engineer the process, applying it to your future. You can look forward as well as back. Today I see "dead ends" and "failures" as intrinsic to the organic process of creating a path of your own.

A tree is the sum total of its experiments in reaching the light, and rarely (if ever) is this effort a straight line from vision to reality. We humans, however, seem to be addicted to the idea that life works (or at least should work) as follows:

Aspirations ———> A Well-Laid Plan ———> Goal Achieved!

I know this kind of thinking has often been applied by me. Many times, I've been disappointed and discouraged because I haven't been able to draw, and then pursue, a straight line from Point A to Point B. Even when I've "known" life is more complicated than that, I've acted as if it weren't.

The prime directive of a tree is to reach the life-giving light. All that apparently crazy, here-there-and-everywhere is in service of the tree's need for sun. And that's why I've changed my thinking, as well as my way of creating a path.

You see, the tree is on to something—and I think I know what it is.

I'm not talking about creating 10 new businesses or launching 50 new projects. I'm not suggesting you should run, willy-nilly, in every direction. That's certainly not what I do. Instead, I focus on activating as many potential trajectories in my life as I can, by nourishing relationships in my life and business. Just as the prime directive of a tree is to reach the life-giving light, my prime directive is to nurture my community, every day.

The second thing I do is to introduce as much variety into my life as I can. I take long showers. I go for walks in the woods. I meet with, and talk to, as many interesting people as I can. When I really need to be productive, I get away from my desk.

Because here is the worst way I've found to be productive:

Sit at Computer ———> Work Eight Hours ———> Get Results

And yet that's still how we see work, as a linear process.

The fact is that we are addicted to straight lines and old ways of doing things. I know how hard it is to let go. I've made painful adjustments. I used to believe in things like:

Go to School ———> Get an Education ———> Work Hard ———> Succeed

or

Get an Agent ———> Find a Publisher ———> Write Books ———> Make Money

or

Get Hired by a Newspaper ———> File Stories ———> Get Paid ———> Retire

None of these things have worked out as advertised. I've only been miserable and unfulfilled pursuing them. It took a painful adjustment, and months of study and effort, to let go of the old ways of thinking. And that was after years of emotional work, gradually getting to the place where I could admit that what I was doing wasn't working—and would never work.

Going in a new direction is hard. You may have a decade invested in that branch of yours. It may be the favorite branch on your tree. Maybe it's the only branch. You probably imagined it soaring one day above the canopy, into the full and glorious life-affirming sun of a new day. But what if it doesn't?

If you build your life on the principle of abundance, each day nurturing a wide network of relationships, being open to many possibilities—sending out many branches—you'll never have this problem. You'll soon realize that your life is, like a tree, the sum total of its trajectories, explorations, and so-called "dead-ends."

A tree, like a life, is nothing less than the sum of its experiments.

Show the World!

"Your brand is what other people say about you when you're not in the room."
– Jeff Bezos, CEO of Amazon

After you've completed the first two sections, here is where all your hard work pays off! You're almost ready to display your unique brilliance to the world in networking conversations, cover letters, through your resume, LinkedIn profile, and in job interviews.

The purpose of this section is to help you take what you've learned about yourself and position it into a clear and intentional brand within your job search materials. You might be as clear as day about who you are and the unique value you can offer, but if it's not clear to others, it's a non-starter.

I strongly encourage you to consistently revisit your YouMap® through every step of this section. It provides a solid starting point to display your unique design by using the language and insights from your profile. It's also a great way to convey a consistent message across your job search materials and LinkedIn profile, or on your website, if you have one.

Consistent messaging is crucial for a strong brand.

Some people have an aversion to the term "personal branding." When I speak of brand, I'm simply referring to the ability to authentically demonstrate who you are and what you can do, which drives home the value you can bring an employer. This makes you more memorable and demonstrates your self-awareness. In short, you come across like you really have it together! The alternative is leaving someone unconvinced or unsure about what you have to offer.

I love the way Dharmesh Shah, HubSpot founder, explains personal branding:

"When a personal brand is an authentic extension of the real person and not an artificial construct, it inspires trust."

Before you set out to show the world, you should first determine your target: those who need most what you do best. Sharing a honed message to a targeted audience will yield better results than taking a willy-nilly, unfocused approach to launching your job search. In short, you need a strategy, so that's where we'll begin.

Targeting Opportunities

When seeking new opportunities, avoid chasing roles. Seek companies you want to work for that will value the contributions you're positioned to bring and that have a culture aligned to your values. Reference your YouMap® as you do your research to align who you are, what you do best, and what you deem most important to the environment you work in.

Do Your Research

Research companies of interest and read what current and former employees say about working there on websites such as Glassdoor.com and Vault.com. While it's true some former, even current, employees write reviews out of revenge for a perceived slight—also known as sour grapes—you can identify consistent cultural themes that might be occurring after reading several reviews. Don't let one negative review scare you away. Every company will have at least one bad review and likely more.

Note and categorize the complaints, such as:

• Communication problems
• Lack of strategy
• Chaotic change management

- Low employee morale
- Lack of promotional opportunities
- Incompetent management
- Culture problems such as gossip, backbiting, and finger-pointing
- Constant turnover or lay-offs
- Scarce training and/or development opportunities
- Low compensation or inadequate benefits
- Poor work/life balance

Also, make note of the positive themes you encounter such as opportunities for growth, a collaborative culture, excellent benefits, and strong leadership.

In addition to online employee feedback, research the company website to learn what they say in posted job descriptions about their culture and search for customer reviews. If customers are treated poorly, you could very well experience the same treatment as an employee. Perform a news search to read stories about companies of interest—anything you can get your hands on. To do this, perform a search in Google and click "News" to filter the results.

How does what you're reading align with your prioritized list of values? Are job descriptions of interest highlighting the strengths and skills you enjoy and are good at, and are they aligned to your interests? Do they describe a culture you'll likely enjoy? For example, if you value fun and vibrant workplace cultures, does that culture come across in their recruiting messaging?

As you review job descriptions at companies that appeal to you, go through and highlight the skills they're looking for, both in the job description and in the motivated skills in your YouMap®. How many of the highlighted skills in the job description did you highlight in your profile? You should refer to your original motivated skills exercise. Note and compare all job descriptions of interest to the burn out and low priority skills you flagged.

Revisit the "My Motivated Skills Insights" section beginning on page 66. Did you capture insights that are helpful as you evaluate the job description? When you first completed your YouMap® you did so impartially, without influence from a specific opportunity. This helps guard against compromising on red flags a role might appear to have. The job description tells a story, both by what's written and what's not. Let me take a moment to explain.

Let's say the job description is just a few sentences, doesn't provide information about what the company values, who you should be, and a clear description of how the role fits into the mission and vision of the company or team. What if it also lacks expectations and deliverables for the position, what a high performer should look like, or perhaps even the challenges and opportunities you might face?

Personally, I view this as a big red flag.

Here are a few possible explanations for insufficient information in a job description:

- Not much thought or importance is placed on their recruiting process.
- The hiring manager is so busy they hurriedly slapped together a job description.
- The hiring manager hasn't taken time to define the needs of the position.
- Someone who doesn't understand the needs of the position wrote the job description.
- The role is new and hasn't been fully thought-out.
- The company is secretive about sharing details for roles in their organization.

None of these reasons position you for success. If the expectations of the role aren't clear, how can your success be clearly measured?

If hiring managers are too busy to put thought to roles they're hiring for, what does that say about what's strategically important to them, or the work/life prioritization of the company?

If the recruiting process and messaging to attract the right people into the right roles of the company isn't of paramount importance, what might that say about the organization's culture?

Other sources of research are informational interviews, which I discussed in detail near the end of the "Blaze Your Path" section. I often ask people (not the same ones repeatedly) if they would be willing to speak to a client who is considering a specific company they are knowledgeable about. In fact, I just did so today before writing this. A former coworker said she would be happy to discuss her experience with a company my client is interested in.

Once you have a short list of company targets, if the employment section of their website has job search alerts, turn them on for roles you're targeting to be notified of available positions. If not, put it on your calendar to check at least once weekly for new postings on their website.

Additionally, note the social media icons on the company's website and follow them across those channels. This is another way to learn about new openings and provides a way to thoughtfully interact with the company and get noticed by adding value to their online content.

Once you've targeted prospects, you need to engage in conversations with people to turn prospects into opportunities.

> **Tip**: Stay focused on the position you're trying to land! Keep your messaging targeted and consistent throughout each of the upcoming sections.

Networking & Informational Interviews

To network effectively and make a strong impression in informational interviews you must learn to develop your competence in networking conversations. This is often referred to as your elevator pitch, but because people don't like to be "pitched" to, I'll refer to this as a networking conversation.

As you target your prospects, you'll want to request informational interviews through your network, engage in formal networking events, and informally network with people you meet as you go about your day.

I am a co-host for LinkedIn Local in Charlotte, NC. You can tell who has taken time to craft an effective networking conversation. Some of the attendees can effortlessly explain what they do, who they serve, and the value they bring.

Others spoke about themselves for a couple of minutes, and I still didn't have a clear sense of what they did, whom they helped, or the value they provided. If you're not familiar, LinkedIn Local is a networking event to meet the people behind the profiles. It gives LinkedIn connections an opportunity to cultivate professional online relationships face-to-face.

Sometimes it's difficult to understand someone's line of work because they use industry jargon that stands in the way of our comprehension. I fall into this trap on occasion myself.

When I first started clarifying my own brand, I spent a lot of time telling people how I helped them. In general, people don't care about the how. I would rattle off all the things I do, all the tools I use. Yawn. Be mindful of this as you craft your message.

My mentor, Steve Lishansky, helped me see a better way. He told me a story about a kitchen contractor. If you decided to renovate your kitchen, whom would you rather hire: contractor number one or contractor number two?

Contractor number one pulls out his tools, shows you each one, and explains how he uses it. He also details how his tools are top-of-the-line and better than those of other contractors.

Contractor number two asks you how you envision your family using this new space and what goals you want to accomplish with your new kitchen design. Will you have family gatherings here? Do you cook and bake regularly? How do you want the space to make you and your family feel when you're in it?

The first contractor is focused on the means. The second, the result. This caused me to rethink the way I position myself in the world. Now, I usually share my "why" and "what" but not the "how" unless asked.

"Do you love Mondays? I help people who are tired of dreading Monday find career satisfaction through five key areas of focus: certifying coaches, career discovery coaching, executive coaching, workshops, and writing books."

Rather than share gory details of my process, my certifications—my "how"—I focus on the problem I solve and the outcome prospective clients want.

When you find yourself in a networking scenario, it's critical to communicate three things:

1. The kind of role (or customers) you're targeting
2. The strengths and experience you bring
3. The value the employer (or customer) will receive

Here are some examples illustrating this approach for different career phases.

Recent Graduate

I'm a recent graduate with a degree in business and I'm seeking a role in digital marketing. While obtaining my degree, I enjoyed my marketing classes most and had the chance to create a social media marketing campaign for a local business as my cornerstone project. Because of the campaign, the business increased their followers by 500% across three platforms and gained seven new clients totaling $120,000 in new business.

Career Transition

I'm an accountant with ten years of experience seeking a process improvement role in a medium-sized financial services company. I recently acquired my Six Sigma Green Belt and transformed the accounting function in my current role through process reengineering and improvements, saving the company $100,000 annually.

Seeking Promotion to Management

I'm a project manager seeking to move into management in the healthcare industry. I've had much success as an individual contributor. However, over the past three years, I've mentored five people in career development resulting in three of those people receiving promotions. My greatest contribution to an employer is my ability to grow and develop people to their greatest potential.

To create your networking conversation, you should expand on the My Unique Contribution statement from your YouMap®. Also, reference your "Strengths Insight Guide," which offers descriptive language about your strengths. The Strengths Insight Guide was introduced in the "Discover Your Strengths" section.

Use the space below to capture your three-part statement, explained above, for your networking conversations. Practice it aloud and tweak it until it feels natural. Remember, you're writing your networking conversation to be spoken.

Kristin A. Sherry   143

Since we don't speak the way we write, you're going to need to edit and rework it until it flows.

_____
_____
_____
_____
_____
_____
_____
_____
_____
_____
_____
_____
_____

After you've practiced aloud, share your networking conversation with a friend or family member for feedback. You never know when a networking opportunity will present itself, so you must always be ready!

The job services site, Workopolis, reports that on average only 2% of applicants are contacted for an interview. Therefore, your most effective strategy is to network into a company to dramatically increase your odds with a personal referral. One of the ways you can stand out in networking is by using a personal networking sheet.

The Personal Networking Sheet

My colleague, Bernie, recently shared a networking document with me that he created to help others support him in his job search. Bernie included the following informational sections in his networking sheet:

- Introduction
- Desired role
- Possible positions
- Summary of professional background
- Strengths and skills

- Highlight of related achievements
- Target companies
- How you might help me

Peruse the image of Bernie's networking sheet below. One thing I like best about his document is the "Possible Positions" section that lists roles that are a good fit for him. This is helpful to those he's networking with because it sparks ideas such as the right people they should introduce to him.

If you're interested in customizing your own networking sheet, Bernie has generously shared his template available for download at MyYouMap.com.

You can send your networking sheet to people in preparation for a networking conversation or take copies with you when networking in person.

Introduction: I'm currently seeking a new job. This "networking sheet" identifies my desired role.

Who in your network would provide input as I search for this role?

Desired Role: I'm driven by a zeal to support and service the business process through programs, projects, and resources that maximize sales opportunity.

Possible Positions

- Special Projects Manager, a trusted staff assistant managing strategic business initiatives on behalf of a manager or director

- Program Manager, implementing strategic business programs that equip sales reps or expand opportunity

- Sales Logistics Coordinator, providing business support for the sales or product delivery process

- Business Systems Consultant, collaborating across functional lines to create synergy between the business unit and the product team

- Business Process Improvement Specialist, improving the business process to achieve sales efficiencies

Summary of Professional Background

1. Cross-functional Experience – Roles in HR, field sales, technical support, corporate marketing, and software development. Technical degree and IT experience

2. Business Operations Exposure – Positions with a Fortune 500 computer corporation, small business, IT/technology start-up, and nonprofit organizations

Strengths and Skills

- Rare combination of relational and analytical abilities—both people and project/planning skills

- Customer-facing skills, creating credibility and rapport that engenders a trusting business relationship

- Strong verbal and written communication skills

- Diligence and dependability

- Thoroughness. Detail-oriented, with an emphasis on quality and excellence

Highlight of Related Achievements

- Earned awards for:

  > Managing the consensus process across five industry marketing teams—a process that established common software requirements for third party applications

  > Salvaging a $200K+ sales order threatened by a parts shortage

  > Writing a guidebook on how to convert and migrate third party software applications from a competitive computer platform

  > Managing a software conversion project

  > Writing a sales plan used as a model plan for peers across the country

- Contributed to millions of dollars in sales as a member of an elite technical support team that delivered: 1) product support 2) sales training 3) customer presentations 4) design consultations and 5) trades how support

- Interfaced with product design and development teams to facilitate 35 field tests in support of sales opportunities

- Managed the design of three medium-to-large scale websites and the design of a CRM database

- Launched a series of full-day training seminars

- Executive Assistant to the Director of a nonprofit organization.

Target Companies

1. Location – South Charlotte, Pineville, Ballantyne, Blakeney, Matthews, Fort Mill, or Rock Hill.

2. Possible Companies – ACME Co., ABC Computers, or companies new to the Charlotte area.

I am appreciative if you are able to...

1. ...introduce me to someone at one of my target companies

2. ...connect me with one or two individuals in your professional or personal network

3. ...share this document with one or two other individuals in your network

Networking on LinkedIn

In addition to a face-to-face networking strategy, you should leverage the power of LinkedIn to identify people for networking conversations to help you access a company from the inside.

I've said it before, and I'll say it again—pursue companies, not jobs. If you've already worked through the "Targeting Opportunities" part of this section, you might already have your desired companies identified. If so, here is how you can use LinkedIn to network into those companies.

Open a browser and go to www.linkedin.com, type the company name in the search box, then hit enter. If there is no other company by the same name, the search will take you directly to the company page. Otherwise, you will need to click the correct company from the list of results.

The screenshot below shows a search result for my company, Virtus Career Consulting. If I want to view everyone who works at Virtus Career Consulting, I can click on "See all 4 employees on LinkedIn" to view the list of employees.

After clicking the link to see all four employees on LinkedIn at Virtus Career Consulting, I receive a list of employees who have Virtus Career Consulting listed as their current or previous employer on their LinkedIn profile:

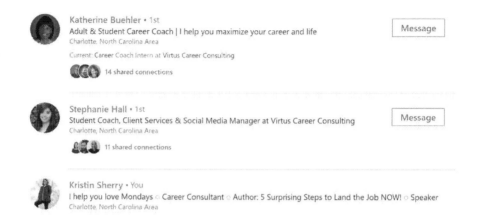

I can now see everyone on LinkedIn who works at Virtus Career Consulting including their job titles, location, and degrees of connection to me. Of course, everyone listed here is a 1st degree connection of mine, which means we are directly connected to each other on LinkedIn.

A 2nd degree connection indicates the person is connected to someone I am directly connected to. If someone is a 3rd degree connection, they are connected to one or more of my second degree connections. Leverage 1st and 2nd degree connections for networking as a priority over third connections unless you have none. Contacting third degree connections is like conducting cold calls. You can certainly engage in cold outreach, but your success rate might be lower.

As you view employees on LinkedIn at your target companies, determine whom you know best and are comfortable sending a message to request a networking conversation. Ideally, you want to contact first degree connections initially because they work directly at your target company. If you're not comfortable contacting your first degree connections, or you don't have any first degree connections, view your second degree connections to see shared first degree connections.

Look again at the previous screenshot and notice where it says "11 shared connections" under Stephanie Hall. If Stephanie were a second degree connection who worked at a company I want to work for, I could click the eleven shared connections hyperlink to view the eleven people I am connected to who are also connected to Stephanie.

I could then write to some of those connections and ask if they would be willing to introduce me to Stephanie.

Here is how you might word a request to a **1st degree** connection who works at your target company.

"I'm writing because I see you currently work at Virtus Career Consulting. [I recently applied for a job | I am interested in this company | I am researching this company as a potential future employer] and would appreciate speaking with you briefly about your experience working there as part of my research on the workplace culture."

Here is how you might word a request to a 2nd degree connection who knows someone at your target company.

"I'm writing because I see you are connected to Stephanie Hall at Virtus Career Consulting. I'd greatly appreciate it if you would introduce me to Stephanie. I'd like to request a brief conversation to discuss her experience working at Virtus Career Consulting as I research the company's culture. If I can do anything for you, or introduce you to anyone in my network, please do not hesitate to ask."

I suggest identifying more than one person to contact. Sometimes people can be unresponsive to their LinkedIn messages so it's good to have a backup. You can also look at the individual's profile to see if their email address is displayed in the upper right-hand corner under Contact and Personal Info to contact them by email. If a user has their email hidden in their privacy settings, the email will not be visible.

Tip: Always personalize your LinkedIn invitations. For example, share why you want to join the person's network.

Once you've identified target roles, desirable companies, have your networking conversation down pat, and maybe even a snazzy new networking sheet, it's time to create the marketing materials that will get you the job!

Ideally, you should have at least your resume and LinkedIn profile ready as you begin networking because the people you are networking with might ask to see your resume. Don't worry, we'll cover all this, and more, in this section.

Employer-Focused Cover Letters

Do people read cover letters? It depends whom you ask. A lot of recruiters will tell you no. When I was a hiring manager in the corporate world, I read every cover letter passed on to me by the recruiter. Your audience for the cover letter is not the recruiter; it's your potential manager.

I read each cover letter because I wanted to make the best hiring decision possible. Why would I ignore another piece of information available to me in making that decision? Recruiters at my company viewed candidates with a different lens than I did.

It's tempting to listen to recruiters tell you not to waste your time but consider this: You will never be penalized for taking the initiative to write a cover letter. If it comes down to you and another candidate, don't let the fact your competitor took time to write a personalized cover letter and you didn't be a deciding factor.

The good news? You've done a lot of legwork for your cover letter in section two, "Blaze Your Path." In the "Targeting Opportunities" section, I showed you how to research companies to determine where you'd most like to work. Then, in the "Networking and Informational Interviews" section, I reviewed creating your three-part value statement. You've already done your research to know why you want to work at the company and how you can bring your skills, strengths, and experiences to deliver value to the employer.

The following information is not meant to provide exhaustive instruction on cover letters. My goal is to provide basic direction and, more importantly, to help you convey an authentic, employer-focused brand message.

Cover Letter Basics

• Use the same font at the top of your cover letter as your resume so they are consistent.

• Include your name, email address and one contact number, preferably a mobile number.

- Limit the length to one page.
- Attempt to find the hiring manager's name to personalize the letter. Contact HR, ask the recruiter, or use LinkedIn to search the company name and job title you might report to.
- Structure the opening paragraph to be employer-focused instead of all about you.
- Leverage your values from your YouMap® to bring shared values to light.
- Connect your motivating skills and experiences to the requirements in the job description.
- Do not simply reiterate your resume. A cover letter should explain why you want to work for them and why you're a good fit for their needs.
- End with a call to action.

Sample Cover Letter

The following cover letter example illustrates five distinct sections of a cover letter:

① – Indicate the position you're applying for either by position title or the Job ID in the job description.

② – Briefly explain why you want to work there. Focus on values you uncovered in the "Discover Your Values" section that align with the employer's values and brand. Make the connection. If you know someone in the company who referred you, mention it here.

③ – Highlight your experiences and the abilities they seek in the job description; this is the value they'll receive. Use language that's consistent with the strengths and motivating skills you've captured in your YouMap®. You could also weave your networking conversation into your cover letter.

④ – Illustrate the kind of workplace or team culture you're looking for and share more about yourself without getting too personal. The values section of your YouMap® contains relevant insights.

⑤ – Call to action. Customize this sentence and invite the hiring manager to contact you by phone or email.

JOHN DOE
john.doe@samplemail.com

(555) 456-7890

11/8/2018

Dear Ms. Jones:

I was pleased to discover ACME Pharmaceuticals is seeking a Territory Business Manager for the Atlanta, GA area. ①

ACME's unwavering compassion for patients and respect for the individual echoes my own values and operating principles. The company's mission to bring life changing therapies to market is admirable. I am a passionate advocate for healthcare professionals and patients and would be proud to launch Mirellus for patients with critical, unmet medical needs. ②

My experience and abilities also strongly match your needs. My background as a trust-building sales representative with analytical abilities and swift clinical mastery—earning numerous awards for clinical knowledge and selling skills—afford me the business-critical context and insight into the lifeblood of our business: our providers and patients. ③

I have deep experience, including eight product launches, turnaround of underperforming territories, provider education and training, managed care and reimbursement, prescriber influence, and managing cross-functional relationships. I recognize patterns and generate new insights, simply explain complex information and findings, persuasively present ideas, and collaborate on solutions. My specialty is tying it all together to convey how a therapy has a meaningful impact on a patient's life.

I value progressive thinking, initiative, teamwork, commitment, and performance. I seek to work within an innovative company such as ACME that shares these values and a drive for success. ④

I reiterate my enthusiasm to join your team and look forward to hearing from you. Please contact me at (555) 123-4567 or john.doe@myemail.com. ⑤

Sincerely,

John Doe

Many other cover letter samples exist online. If you use one, remember to weave your own authentic brand into the template using your YouMap® insights, begin the letter with an employer focus, and make intentional connections between you and the employer through your strengths, shared values, and experience.

Don't be daunted by what might seem to be a disproportionately large section of this book. Resumes are undoubtedly the most stressful exercise for job seekers, so I've decided to give this topic its due attention. What you're about to read is chock full of great advice, examples, and tips!

One of the most frustrating experiences for job seekers is the varied and inconsistent information surrounding resumes. Even the simple topic of resume page length continues to be a subject of debate. Also important to note is that resumes vary widely in different countries.

For example, it's common for a picture to be included on a resume in many parts of the world, yet this is not recommended in the United States or Canada due to employment discrimination laws. Also, in the US, a CV (Curriculum Vitae) is a term largely reserved for academic resumes, yet CV is a preferred term in many countries.

Resume writing is both an art and a science, therefore, some advice is merely opinion. There are, however, many agreed upon best practices, although not all advice is a best practice for all industries. Feeling confused, yet?

Don't worry! I've invited additional experts in the career services industry to add their advice and tips to this book to help you make sense of the noise.

In cases where our resume experts have a difference of opinion or approach, you can choose your preferred option and take comfort in the fact it's a preference more than a rule.

Tackling your own resume can be a challenging and trying exercise. Therefore, if you're in the market to hire a resume writer, I've included the contact information for the experienced writers who have contributed to this book in Tools & Resources.

The first question you must ask before tackling your resume is, "What position(s) am I targeting with my resume?" The main goal of the first two sections of this book was to help you answer this question.

I had a former client who insisted upon keeping his options open when job searching. He wanted to keep his resume and LinkedIn profile general for "broad appeal."

The only thing a generalized, untargeted resume will bring is practice shots on the hiring manager's trash can with YOUR resume. One of the best practices most resume writers agree on is this: If you market yourself to everyone, you will end up appealing to no one.

If you aren't certain of your target, you can go back through the "Blaze Your Path" section.

The next question is really a cluster of related questions, "What organizations or companies do I intend to target? What is their culture like? What are their needs, and how can I add value to this company through the position I'm targeting?" Your YouMap® can help you answer this last question—specifically, with your My Unique Contribution statement.

Next, ask, "What are the skills, experiences, characteristics, and strengths they are seeking in the job description that my resume should include? What do I do better than other people in this kind of role?" Hint: Think of your strengths revealed in the "Find Yourself" section.

I asked resume writers and job search strategists Patricia Edwards, Kerri Twigg, and Kamara Toffolo to share their approach to writing resumes to help you transform your resume from weak to wow!

Each writer has a distinct style with advice that progressively builds on the last writer's advice. We'll start with the prework and questions you must ask yourself, then dig into storytelling, and finally conduct a section-by-section walkthrough of resume construction. This section is a goldmine with something for everyone.

Tip: Read Patricia, Kerri, and Kamara's bios in Tools & Resources to learn a bit more about them before reading their advice.

The following pages contain advice based on Patricia, Kerri, and Kamara's extensive resume writing expertise and the most important information they think you should know.

First, we'll hear from Patricia Edwards.

Patricia's mission is to educate, inspire, and empower job seekers to land their ideal role. How does she do that? With more than twenty-five years of experience recruiting, interviewing, hiring and developing professionals in previous roles as a senior human resources and talent manager, she is well equipped.

Patricia recommends a series of five reflection questions, which she shares here to help you develop the right frame of mind as you begin writing your resume.

Focusing Your Resume through Reflection by Patricia Edwards

The conversations I have with job seekers are not really different from those I had with the employees of Fortune 100 and 200 companies I supported to hire and retain top talent. I typically ask these five questions in my initial consultation.

If we were talking one year from now, what would be different, what would you be doing, what would be the environment, with whom would you be working, what role would you have and how would you know you were successful and fulfilled?

These questions get at the heart of what the job seeker is striving to find in his or her ideal work world. It is also a stretch for some to be able to articulate those desires, values, and goals in a more tangible way.

**Describe one of your best days at work
and one of your worst days at work.**

This question is designed to quickly understand what makes the person feel successful, valued, and recognized, as well as the drivers behind the desire for a career change. Perhaps he wants to use natural gifts and talents more often. Perhaps it is a matter of a bad culture fit or a poor work relationship with his manager, peers, or clients.

What are your top three career achievements?

This question is an eye-opener for many, and I am surprised at the number of high level professionals who cannot think of more than one achievement. That tells me they are either beaten down from not getting recognition for their contributions, or they are not aware of their successes. So, we need to drill down to the achievements I know they have accomplished so they can articulate these on their resumes, as well as their LinkedIn profiles and, most importantly, in interviews.

If I were to ask your manager or colleagues what your top five strengths are, what would they tell me?

I often get the deer in the headlights look initially; however, after a few moments, I help the individual inventory what she does easily, naturally, and well. This is a critical self-assessment to communicate her value and stand out against the competition in the job market. My work with emotional intelligence coaching has assisted me with coaching clients in self-awareness, realistic thinking, and positivity when viewing their strengths.

If you were given a going away or retirement party, how would you want to be remembered by those with whom you worked? What would you want them to say about you?

This question reveals the person's career and life values and ultimately what matters most to them. Few people consider this question, especially younger people. It is derived from a principle in the great book, The 7 Habits of Highly Effective People. Begin with the end in mind.

Much of the language above, such as strengths and values, should be very familiar to you by now. These questions can help you refine the direction and focus you take with your resume. Based on the answers to these questions, you'll want to focus on skills and accomplishments that have motivated you and values that are most important to you.

Your answers to the above questions should also be instructive on what not to include in your resume. You don't want to attract opportunities that use your burnout skills, will not capitalize on your strengths, or violate your values.

Tip: Keep your YouMap® close at hand as you prepare the first draft of your resume to ensure you are representing your deal makers well with your skills and accomplishments, while avoiding your deal breakers by not including skills and accomplishments that demotivate you.

Now, what if you want to change careers?

I could share hundreds of examples as inspiration. Here are some real client examples of career transitions. If they did it, you can too.

- Lawyer to corporate communications manager
- Personal banker to real estate analyst
- Mortgage processor to executive assistant
- Marketing specialist to branding strategist
- Sales manager to financial advisor
- Restaurant manager to training and development manager
- Quality assurance specialist to human resources generalist
- Communications specialist to instructional designer
- Marketing manager to adjunct professor
- Travel agent to customer services manager
- Chemical engineer to organizational development manager
- High school English teacher to content writer

Once your career direction is clear after working through the first two sections of this book, you can follow these steps to approach your resume.

Step 1: Set the current resume aside and start fresh!

Step 2: Disregard the chronological resume format. Use a functional resume format, placing emphasis on "Accomplishments" and "Skills" sections at the top of the resume.

Step 3: Base the new resume on the position being pursued and use the job posting or description as a resource. Include your identified transferable skills and experiences. Current and past job titles are not relevant—strengths and achievements are.

Angela is one client who changed career paths.

Angela's Story

Angela was an elementary teacher whose second home was a museum.

She came to me completely burned-out from teaching second graders for twenty years. She loved the interaction with youngsters but was fed up with all the administrative responsibilities. When I asked her to imagine herself in a perfect role, she immediately smiled and said, "I have always seen myself as either a librarian or as an educator in a museum and teaching children."

Her love for children and teaching came through—loud and clear.

We researched her options and located a few museum educator positions. I customized Angela's resume so it would be keyword rich and achievement-based. Then we tackled her LinkedIn profile, where she connected with recruiters and directors of museums to manage a children's science museum on the west coast.

Angela's story is certainly inspiring! I (Kristin) agree with Patricia that if Angela can do it, you can too. I specialize in career transition and have clients who were told by recruiters it would not be possible for them to transition from their current career to their new career target. Yet they have. The recruiters were partially right—transitioning to a new career is much less likely if you present yourself in your current package. It's all about how you position yourself!

Next, you'll hear from storyteller extraordinaire, Kerri Twigg. Kerri will help you develop a different frame of mind as you consider how you want to showcase yourself in your resume as she teaches you to authentically tell your story.

Kerri began her career in the arts where she worked as a drama instructor and playwright, both of which inform her coaching methods. Stories are powerful, and Kerri is an expert who can help you capture and hold the attention of those who read your resume.

Your Resume Tells a Story by Kerri Twigg

I'm romantic about resumes. I think they are the single most important document in a professional's life, which is sad, considering the state of many people's resumes. It doesn't need to be that way.

Before I meet with people about resume development, I have them do two things.

Use Index Cards

First, buy a package of index cards. Write down an accomplishment story from your career every day on a card, one per day, for the next seven to ten days. Some people can take these instructions and run with them; others need a few prompts. Here are some prompts I recommend.

Write down a story about a time you helped a coworker.

What was the biggest impact you had on an organization?

When did you have flow at work, where it seemed that time stopped and this flow allowed a great thing to happen?

Tell me about a time you left work feeling awesome about what you did that day. It can be teeny or huge. Describe that day.

List Jobs That Attract You

Next, I ask clients to find and send me three to five positions they are attracted to. It doesn't mean they have to apply for the jobs. I am looking for clues about what their desired job includes. Often people will select job descriptions where they don't even want to work, but they want to sound like the kind of person who has that job. I use the job advertisement as a map to explore other stories with my clients. I take apart the job ads, find common elements, and send a list of questions related to those job ads to my clients.

You can do this yourself by selecting three to five ads you are drawn to. Look for common words, phrases, or ideas. What do you like about that word, phrase, or idea? Why would you thrive in that environment? What words from that ad could you start weaving into your everyday language so it becomes a part of who you are?

Leave Your Comfort Zone

I work this way because job search requires laser focus and strong targets the further you get into it. Job seekers try to blend in and make a safe resume from the beginning. Safe resumes don't get read. If I can work with a client from their core stories and find their transferable skills, we can play with a lot of input as we develop the resume. We aren't starting the process from a limited place. We are starting from a possibilities view.

> **Tip**: If you have followed Kristin's career exploration process, look at your preferred, motivated skills and write down stories about each of those pieces for this part of the process.

Working with Stories

After the stories are down and clients have answered additional questions relating to the job postings they shared, we have a meeting. During this meeting, I ask them to share their stories aloud with me so I can get a feel for their language. I use this to write their resume.

I am a playwright and see each client as a character. Their objective is to land a certain kind of job where they get to use their top skills in their ideal environment. Everything needs to sound like them. I think one danger in hiring a resume writer is that you can feel that the resume looks great, but it needs to look great and sound like you because you are the person going to the interview, not your resume writer. Your stories are the foundation of your job search.

You can do this on your own by recording yourself talking. You can even speak out your entire resume and then edit it into accomplishment statements.

Keystone Resume System

My favorite way to work with resumes is to create a keystone resume. This is where all your stories, job postings, education and community involvement go into one master document. This document might be ten pages long to include all your accomplishments. The keystone resume is a living document, so once you have created it, you can keep adding to it for your entire career.

For example, if I had three stories about helping a client, I would add them to my keystone resume:

Story A: Story about helping a client with a resume

Story B: Story about driving through a snowstorm to help prep someone for an interview

Story C: Story about a client who got a 40% salary increase based on the resume

I add categories to my keystone resume and then when a job comes up, I choose the best story to tell them. For example, if a job came up with Virtus Career Consulting, I would think about the values and personalities of the people on their team. I think they would be most impressed by the driving through the snowstorm story, so that is one story I would choose to tell.

If a university were hiring someone to teach resume writing, I would choose Story A.

After you have all your stories down, it gets easy to select the right ones to share each time.

Here's how.

When a job comes up that you want to apply for, you look at:

• What the company says they want
• What words they keep using that you'll want to integrate
• What angle you'll highlight in your resume

Then, using that lens, select stories from your keystone resume to populate an ultra-focused resume for the position. You choose stories that company will care about based on your research on the role and reading the job ad. You just copy and paste the stories over to your resume, play around with the summary to make sure it is a match, and you're done.

Throughout your career, keep an email folder called "great job" and save any thank you letters or words of praise in it. Schedule time every quarter to add new material to your resume, and you will always be prepared. Chance favors the prepared!

From Weak to Wow

While the keystone resume creates a great system, the core content still needs to be great. You can move a resume from weak and ignored to people saying,

"Whoa, wow, they are perfect!" with just a few changes.

- Always tailor your resume. I am not joking. Always tailor it. The payoff is worth it.
- Know your angle before you start writing. Decide on what you want to emphasize and stick to the script. You are not trying to tell the hiring person EVERYTHING. You are trying to tell them enough to get them to call you. Save something for the interview rounds.
- Show personality. You don't need to crack jokes in your summary but give a taste of your soft skills and how you work, instead of all facts.
- But not too soft. While soft skills are necessary, having numbers to back up your work adds tremendous value.
- Do the ex-test. If an ex-partner or friend saw this resume, would you be proud? Does it sound like you and celebrate your best career accomplishments? If you feel shame about it, keep working. Your resume should be something you are proud and eager to send people.
- Check the flow of the document by acting it out. Read each section and act out the punctuation. Walk as you read the words, come to a full stop at periods, and hang a leg in the air with commas. Does the resume have flow, or is it a bunch of short choppy sentences? Play around with sentence length and structure to ensure it is enjoyable to read.

Next, we'll hear from Kamara Toffolo as she walks you through the anatomy of an amazing resume!

The Anatomy of an Amazing Resume by Kamara Toffolo

Just like when you're trying to find the best chocolate chip cookie recipe, when you ask your peers and colleagues for advice on resumes, you'll get varied responses.

"Add pecans!" says one friend. "No, never add pecans. Add extra brown sugar," says another. The advice you receive for resumes will be even more diverse.

At the most basic level, a resume is a marketing document. It sells your unique value while also telling your story.

In this section, I will dispel some ambiguity, clear up some myths, and discuss a few best practices for writing a resume that stands out from the crowd and gets noticed.

Stop Sweating Applicant Tracking Systems

The two most common resume questions I receive from job seekers are:

1. How do I work with the Applicant Tracking Systems?
2. What template should I use?

My answer to both of these questions is always: Keep it simple.

In a nutshell, an Applicant Tracking System (ATS) is software used by hiring professionals to make the job application review process more efficient. But efficiency for employers means fear, worry, and confusion for job seekers.

Many job seekers get too hung up on the ATS and beating the bots, so to speak. If your job search strategy lives and dies by the ATS, it's time to reassess. Nothing beats the bots like solid relationships and investing your time and energy in human connection.

There's a lot we can't know about how the ATS is used at any given employer. What we do know is that keywords and structure matter.

To uncover appropriate keywords, analyze job postings and identify the skills that strike you as important. List the skills you have in your skills section (more on this later).

This brings us to the next point—templates.

Pretty Templates Aren't Your Friend

You've probably seen them on Pinterest or possibly Instagram—really aesthetically-pleasing resume templates that use colors, borders, panels, or more. But that's all these templates are: easy on the eyes. Don't fall into the trap and invest in a template just because it looks good.

ATSs have difficulty digesting over-designed resume templates and the designs detract from the content and important information.

In today's competitive job market, a clean and simple resume layout is critical. Statistically speaking, your resume has six seconds in front of a hiring professional for an initial review to determine whether to interview you or send your resume to File 13 (read: the trash).

So, what does clean and simple look like? Let's dive into some detail.

General Structure: Two Pages or Bust

I believe that resumes should not exceed two pages. Page limits on a resume shouldn't be seen as stifling but giving you structure. Even CEO resumes I've written fit comfortably in this structure. A page limit helps you prioritize what's important to include and what's not.

Where I deviate from this rule of thumb is when the job seeker has work experience of five years or fewer. If you have only a few years' work experience, just use one page. Hiring managers appreciate brevity!

If you're having trouble trying to polish a dated resume, stop! Earlier, Patricia recommended starting fresh with your resume and for me this was, well, a breath of fresh air. Trying to iterate a resume that you drafted when you were graduated from college, now as a senior manager, just doesn't fly—especially if you're making a transition. Scrap the old—it probably wasn't working for you anyway—and start anew.

Resume Header: Call Me Maybe? Make Contacting You Foolproof

The first text to grace your resume should be your name, followed by your contact information. There should be easy access to your contact information, which includes:

1. **Your location**: City or metro and state or province will do. There's no need for your full snail mail address.
2. **Phone number**: Include only one number if you have multiple, but make sure it's the one that you're most likely to answer and that it also has voicemail.
3. **Email**: Level up by hyperlinking your email address to give a reviewer a one-click option to email you.
4. **LinkedIn Profile**: Most recruiters use LinkedIn to source candidates. Make finding your profile easy for them.

Tip: For help with hyperlinking an email and LinkedIn profile, check out my video on this topic: https://youtu.be/biEKkjPoq-U

While you have a handy header option in word processing software, you don't want to use it for your resume header. Let me explain.

Resume headers should go in the body of your resume to accommodate our friend, the ATS, to ensure that your contact information is processed. Sometimes an ATS has difficulty reading information embedded in the header section of a document.

Here is an example:

KAMARA TOFFOLO

Toronto, ON	(555) 123-4567
https://ca.linkedin.com/in/kamarat	kamara@kamaratoffolo.com

Another detail you can indicate in your header is any willingness to relocate or any relocation plans or preferences, especially if you're applying from outside of the job posting's city, state, province, or even country. They'll know that you're committed to moving, if needed.

Professional Summary: Tell Them About Yourself (Short and to the Point!)

After your contact information, you should include a brief paragraph that summarizes who you are as a professional. This is where you get to use adjectives to describe your strengths. A frequent hang-up for job seekers when they're trying to write a professional summary section is that it often can feel boastful. But rather than trying to self-describe how amazing you are, include what others have said about you.

Patricia posed the question, "If I were to ask your manager or colleagues what your top five strengths are, what would they tell me?" This is a brilliant question in the way it's framed. By asking the question this way, although the answers are coming from you, they are validated through an external lens and sometimes reflective of actual feedback you've received. This allows you to dig deeply into your self-awareness and powerfully uncover how awesome you really are!

Here are some professional summary examples:

Career Transition

In this example, the summary explains the return to school to obtain an additional degree, yet specifies any transferable skills from the individual's past positions that match the needs of the desired role.

PROFESSIONAL SUMMARY

Aspiring Organizational Development Consultant and current Master of Arts in Industrial/Organizational Psychology candidate (graduating in August 2018). Excited to contribute 10+ years' experience and expertise in finance, strategy, modeling, and analytics and deep understanding of organizational development to support financial services organizations with building robust Learning and Development programs. Known for combining a strong data analysis orientation with quick rapport and relationship-building skills to partner with key stakeholders and deliver results.

Recent College Graduate

In this example, the summary emphasizes academic credentials and areas of strengths. Internship or coursework can also be emphasized if work experience is lacking.

PROFESSIONAL PROFILE

Recent Finance and M.I.S. graduate and aspiring Financial Analyst. Known for analytical acumen, curiosity, and eye for detail. Inquisitive researcher with strength in equity analysis and integrating information to solve complex problems or uncover new understanding. Multilingual communicator, fluent in spoken English, Mandarin, and Spanish, with international experience working overseas as a Finance Intern in Beijing, China.

Lateral Career Move

The individual in this example is seeking a lateral move in operations management. The emphasis is on this individual's experience, which matches the requirements in the job description.

CAREER PROFILE

People-and profit-focused Operations Manager with 15 years' experience building innovative processes that add efficiency to operations. Cross-functional collaborator and mentoring leader who invests in team members' development and success. Data-driven professional, recognized for top performance and proficiency with forecasting, as well as performance and operations reporting.

Technical, Promotional

This individual is seeking a promotion to a more senior role. The emphasis is on her relevant transferable skills and is less focused on the technical skills of an individual contributor. Note the increased emphasis on higher level skills and leadership, as well as illustrating her experience with a larger scope of responsibility.

Some additional sources of positive, professional descriptors for your professional summary can be found in performance appraisals and emails from managers, peers, and clients that praise your dedication and hard work.

I encourage you to be proactive about noting your accomplishments and start keeping a "Kudos" document. It doesn't matter where you keep this document, though I do suggest a cloud-based service that is accessible across all devices such as Google Docs or Evernote. This makes it quick and easy to record achievements when they happen, or even when you recall them, no matter where you are (except the shower, I do not condone phone or computer use there!).

What goes in this Kudos file? all the outstanding things that you've done on the job

This includes:

- Tangible, quantifiable results and how you made them happen
- Great feedback you've received from clients, managers, or even your own direct reports
- Anything you're proud of achieving

Skills and Qualifications: Give Them What They're Looking For

Skills. Qualifications. Areas of Expertise. However you slice it, this is where you really want to match up the skills the employer is seeking from the ideal candidate with the skills and experience you bring to the table.

How do you know what the employer wants? They tell you in their job postings.

Leverage job postings the way Patricia and Kerri noted earlier. Look for keywords and skills that stand out, are frequently stated, and/or are prioritized (listed first or early) in the job posting. You can then take your research findings and align your skills with what the employer needs.

When it comes to skills, you're aiming to list skills in your resume without additional description because what you're really going after are keywords. Avoiding assessment of your own skills is best, as you can't measure them objectively. This also means you need to drop any graphics or icons that show a visual measure of your expertise in a skill.

Here are some examples of how to identify keywords for your skills to include on your resume:

Skill	Keyword
Strategic Problem Solver	Strategy
Good Customer Service Skills	Customer Service
Creating Budgets	Budget Management or Budget Planning

I often see "Excellent Communication Skills" included on resumes, but this is not ideal. There are two main problems with this approach:

1. You're subjectively evaluating your own skill level, which you don't want to do.
2. Recruiters/hiring managers assume you have communication skills.

Don't waste resume space on skills that lack impact. Instead, focus on specialized skills that pack a bigger punch.

The resume structure in which you list your skills need not be complicated. Some resumes use a columned approach. Some include a list that's centered and uses more of the page width. Avoid text boxes or tables to remain compatible with ATSs.

I recommend customizing your skill list each time you submit your resume to a new job to ensure it is tailored to the employer's needs.

Here are two examples of Skills & Qualifications sections:

SKILLS & QUALIFICATIONS

Multi-Product Portfolio Management	IT Operations	Cross-Functional Team Leadership
Program / Product Management	Agile	Relationship Building
Software Development Lifecycle (SDLC)	Stakeholder Management	Client Support
Business Intelligence	Vendor Management	Training
Data Analytics	Resource Allocation	Innovation
Strategic Planning	Product Design	Negotiation

Tip: Add a space before and after a slash (/) such as IT Operations / Quality Assurance. Putting a space before and after the slash ensures the ATS can read and parse two separate skills.

Professional Experience: Show Them the Value You've Created

The Professional Experience section is the largest section of your resume, often representing half of your resume's total real estate. Its prominence requires a great deal of attention, care, and strategy.

Write your Professional Experience section with two core objectives in mind:

1. Giving context to the roles you've held
2. Highlighting accomplishments and results

Simple Structure

When building my clients' Professional Experience sections, I use a simple, consistent structure with the following formatting:

1. On the left margin, enter the position title, with the organization name, city, and state (or province) listed below

2. On the right margin, enter the date range of employment.

3. A brief paragraph to discuss responsibilities and scope of role to provide context comes next.

4. Then provide a few bullets to highlight quantifiable accomplishments, results, and achievements.

It'll look like this:

Assistant to the Regional Manager
Acme Paper Company | Scranton, PA

Description
Description
Description

- *Accomplishment*
- *Accomplishment*
- *Accomplishment*

Describing your role doesn't need to be complicated. Rather than copying and pasting a job description, describe responsibilities that might be unique or unusual to the role or sought-after duties you share with target job postings.

Watch your words. If you're using profession-specific terminology, make sure it resonates across the industry and across all organizations. Resumes that are rife with acronyms and technical terminology can fall flat quickly.

Accomplishments: Amplify Your Strengths

Accomplishments back up the skills and expertise you've included in your resume while also backing up work you love to do. Remember the motivated skills you pinpointed in your YouMap® discovery work? Think about how you leveraged those skills. Your burnout skills, on the other hand, should get no attention on your resume.

When you're determining what accomplishments to include, revisit your Kudos file. Or, use Kerri's stellar suggestion to use index cards to record accomplishments! This approach eases the daunting task of recalling important details by recording bite-size, digestible steps over seven to ten days.

When you're ready to start writing accomplishments in your resume, use bullets to draw attention to these noteworthy achievements. The bullets should lead with the main achievement or result. When possible, include numbers like dollars and percentages.

Quantifying Your Accomplishments: Give Them Your Digits

When you consider what accomplishments make the cut on your resume, prioritize quantifiable ones.

Using numbers to illustrate impact is powerful. Numbers on your resume are essential because they quantify impact.

Here's how:

Without Quantifying:

- Orchestrated shipping of a high volume of paper products to clients across Lackawanna County.

What is high volume to this candidate? How large is Lackawanna County? How many clients do they have?

With Quantifying:

- Orchestrated shipping of 10,000+ paper product orders to 250+ corporate clients across a 465 square mile territory.

See the difference?

For unquantified bullets, put the impact front and center. Some good scenarios to turn into resume accomplishments are:

- Earning a promotion
- Helping someone else earn a promotion (preferably a direct report)
- Building a new process adopted by other departments
- Shifting culture toward one that's more client/service/delivery focused
- Eliminating or minimizing risk exposure
- Repairing relations between departments

Here are some examples:

- Mentored two direct reports over a six-month period; both received promotions within six months
- Appointed as trusted "go-to" person to handle deal forecasting for complex Fortune 500 deals
- Recovered relationship with a client by uncovering a key problem and overcoming their skepticism
- Worked with external customers to resolve an ongoing sales reporting discrepancy

In some cases, even accomplishments that don't appear to be quantifiable can be.

Here is an example:

Before

- Participated in a year-long emerging leader program

After

- Selected as 1 of 10 out of 280 applicants for a year-long emerging leader program

In all cases, with or without numbers, the *how* is really important.

Career Change Accomplishments

When you're writing accomplishments for your resume, the goal is to illustrate your experience for the role in question.

For example, if you're currently a sales representative and one of your accomplishments is:

Grew Scranton territory by 25% in only 18 months through emphasis on printer and tablet cross-selling

Then, let's say through the YouMap® process you identified a different role that is a better fit for you, like an accountant. An ability to grow a territory through influence likely isn't a sought-after skill. But the ability to uncover the opportunity to cross-sell additional products is. It reveals that you're analytical and strategic, both valued transferable skills that would apply to a future role as an accountant.

So, your accomplishment could be reworded like this:

Identified new revenue stream resulting in a 25% increase in sales by analyzing historical sales data and trends to uncover high-potential opportunity

In short, make your accomplishments relevant to your target roles.

Education: Communicate Your Commitment to Learning

Education isn't just a piece of paper. It can be the foundation on which you build your skills or keep those skills up-to-date.

For an experienced professional, the Education section should be the last, or nearly the last, portion of your resume. For new or recent graduates, I advise leading with your Education (after the Summary and Skills sections) as it's typically the most applicable to your current career direction.

When you're listing your education, you want to lead with the credential itself, then the school, and include the graduation date on the right margin (similar to Professional Experience).

It'll look something like this:

Bachelor of Arts in Economics
University Name | City, State/Province

When I work with clients who are concerned about their ages, I remove the graduation date. Education is valuable, but its value is eclipsed by work experience.

Didn't Graduate College? Don't Worry.

I've worked with many clients who started a university degree but put their education on hiatus for all sorts of reasons. How do you address this on a resume?

Let's say you started a degree in accounting and left university in your third year. Was all your studying for naught? Not exactly.

This is how I'd capture it:

Coursework in Accounting
University Name | City, State/Province

That's it!
This approach achieves a couple of things:

1. It does justice to your studies by including it on your resume.
2. It doesn't raise a red flag that you didn't complete it.

Omit Obsolete Credentials

As you've learned, you need to build your resume with your target role in mind. The Education section is no different. It's best to eliminate any credentials that aren't relevant to the job you want. For example, will your old Nortel certification help you land a job as a CIO? Probably not. Axe what doesn't add value.

Get Your Credentials Checked for Equivalency

Different countries equal different education standards. When immigrating to a different country, it's helpful to have your education assessed for equivalency. (Note: There are other benefits and requirements related to the immigration process.)

By having your education equivalency assessed, you anticipate and proactively answer a question that will likely be asked by a recruiter or hiring manager.

In Canada, you can check for Government-approved Education Credential Assessment organizations here: tinyurl.com/ya952klw
In the U.S., you can check here: tinyurl.com/y98epfws

Community Involvement: Exhibit Your Dedication to Giving Back

Community Involvement or Volunteering sections add a boost to your resume. However, this won't make or break your resume. It's more of a nice-to-have than a necessity.

Ensure the content you're including is not too dated. That semester you volunteered for your high school basketball team selling hot dogs and popcorn at their concession stand probably shouldn't make the cut. But the school board or city council you served on a couple of years back, should.

My rule of thumb is to include volunteer work from the past five years.

I'd list volunteer work as follows:

Fundraising Volunteer
Organization Name | City, State/Province

There's no need to get into a lot of detail unless the volunteer work was done during a career gap, in which case you can leverage your involvement as work experience.

If you have only one instance of volunteering in the past five years and it was for less than six months, I wouldn't include it. This kind of singular experience stands out like a sore thumb and could lead to questions you don't want. Why was it so brief? Why just one volunteer role? Did you take this volunteer role solely to beef up your resume?

Personality: Highlight How Human You Are

At the beginning of this section, I said your resume is a marketing document. It sells your unique value and tells your story. This means that showcasing your personality on your resume is an absolute must. But your resume doesn't need to be casual for you to sound like a cool coworker. There's room on your resume for personality *and* professionalism.

Use active language and action verbs to create more of a visual in readers' minds.

For instance, *"Initiated a company-wide health and fitness program, achieving 90% employee involvement in Year 1"* sounds a whole lot more exciting than *"Responsible for helping peers adopt healthier lifestyles."*

Avoid using words you don't normally use, simply because you've seen these terms on other resumes. Also, varied word choices help limit overuse. Don't be afraid to refer to a thesaurus!

Finally, have fun writing your resume and reflecting upon all the incredible results you've created throughout your career. Remember, your story and journey are yours alone, and they have allowed you to make a unique impact at organizations, amongst peers and teams, as well as with clients.

Now, let's hear from Lisa Jones on how Academic Curriculum Vitae (CV) formats differ from industry resumes that have been the focus to this point.

The Academic CV by Lisa Jones

Academic CVs differ from resumes because they are comprehensive documents. As previously mentioned, there is no magic formula for resumes, and the same holds true for a CV. However, a few critical differences are necessary to appeal to higher education positions including teaching positions, deans, and other lead faculty positions.

When applying for higher level education jobs, include all parts of a resume along with the critical sections listed below.

Statement of Teaching Philosophy

This is the first section of your CV and should tell the reader why you want to teach (your passion), how you feel teaching will help shape future practitioners, what tools you'll use to help reach students and keep them engaged (technology, discussion groups, etc.), and your educational theory (pedagogy).

Courses Taught

All courses you have taught should be listed with brief descriptions. Any teaching/training from your professional work experience in industry positions and the military should be listed in this section.

Publications, Conferences, Research

Because CVs are meant to be comprehensive, I suggest listing all your work in these areas to show the depth of your knowledge. You are writing for an academic audience so it is best to use APA format for each of these sections (Visit apastyle.org for more on APA format). Leave out items that don't pertain to your subject matter expertise and those that are outdated.

Highly Competent Subject Areas

This section is listed at the end of your CV and should include the following:

LMS (Learning Management Systems)

List the all the systems you are familiar with as a teaching professional and student. Examples: Moodle, Desire2Learn (D2L), WebEx, and Blackboard.

Software

List the on-premise and web-based technology in your Personal Learning Environment (PLE). If your goal is to teach online, some courses come pre-coded, and others will require you to build or add additional online learning material.

Subject Matter Expertise

List at least fifteen courses you are qualified to teach. These will include courses you have previously taught and those for which you have significant subject matter expertise.

References

References are not listed on resumes but are included on a CV. Try to use references with a higher level of education when applying to higher level education institutions. If you hold a Master's degree, list someone with a PhD.

These are a few sections and tips to help you build a winning CV. Keep in mind, CVs are comprehensive and the page length guidelines differ from resumes.

My hope is that most of your resume questions have been addressed. If you feel overwhelmed at the thought of writing your own resume, don't have time, or lack the motivation, consider hiring a professional resume writer to save you some time and frustration.

All-Star LinkedIn Profiles

This section provides the information you need to create an all-star LinkedIn profile. If you don't have a LinkedIn profile, I exhort you to create one, especially if you want to be found by recruiters. Recruitingbrief.com reports that 65% of LinkedIn's revenue comes from recruiters looking for talent, and more than 90% of recruiters use LinkedIn to source candidates for positions.

According to Jobvite, 60% of recruiters believe culture fit is of highest importance when deciding to recruit and hire candidates (Read more at tinyurl.com/y9bfg26s). Your LinkedIn profile is a great place to showcase your personality and values—much more so than your resume.

Tip: Your LinkedIn profile should not simply reiterate your resume; a LinkedIn profile is not an online resume. Your profile is essentially a digital marketing platform, and you're the featured product!

From a branding standpoint, the three most important parts of your LinkedIn profile are your photo, your headline, and your summary. I will share a simple formula to create your LinkedIn headline and summary, and then Donna Serdula, author of *LinkedIn Profile Optimization for Dummies*, will share her top tips for optimizing your profile and cranking up your job search!

Finally, Lisa Jones will provide a basic overview of some of the other LinkedIn profile sections Donna and I did not cover.

Let's get started!

LinkedIn Headline

Your headline is your what. What do you do better than most people? Your My Unique Contribution statement in your YouMap® is a good starting point to craft your LinkedIn headline. You can pull out key words from your strengths and skills you enjoy as descriptive qualifiers.

> **Tip**: If you're a career changer, I recommend branding your LinkedIn profile for where you're trying to go, not where you are now. If you don't have any experience, you can craft a headline that showcases the top three transferable skills and strengths you have that best relate to your target position. Use ideal or target job descriptions as inspiration. What skills and phrases are used repeatedly in job descriptions that appear to be in high demand and are true of your skills or strengths?

Let's look at an example for an operations process improvement consultant. The headline for this individual will contain her title, some key skills or functional areas, and what she does best.

Sample Headline:
Operations Consultant | Six-Sigma Black Belt | Process Engineering | I maximize call center operation results

The key words and functional skills listed in her headline should resonate with job descriptions she's interested in because the headline is searchable; therefore, she should seek to be found by the key words recruiters will most likely use in searches for people in her field. Make sure to include functional skills and areas of focus you enjoy and want to attract in your key words.

> **Tip**: At the time of this writing, LinkedIn imposes a 120-character limit for a headline and a 2,000-character limit for the summary. Also, the "|" character (referred to as a "pipe") shown in the previous sample headline is located above the Enter key on the right side of your keyboard.

LinkedIn Summary

Your summary is your why and how and should be more personable than your resume. Again, your LinkedIn profile is not an online resume. It might have started out that way, but LinkedIn is continuously evolving.

Here is a simple four-part formula for writing a LinkedIn summary:

1. A brief introductory paragraph expanding on the one thing in your headline you do best (focus on the core problem you solve; the why)
2. Proof to back it up in either a "Select Accomplishments" section or through a brief story that demonstrates what you do best; your how.
3. A call to action (optional) to request people connect with or contact you.
4. Key word summary of skills you enjoy and want to attract. It's important to add key words in your summary as it is searchable, just like the headline.

Sample Four-Part LinkedIn Summary

Many moving parts, processes, and people participate in call center operations. The biggest problem I've seen in my 10+ years working in Operations Process Re-Engineering are the silos that create redundant processes and gaps that swallow up your customers. I help you see the big picture, close gaps, and delight—instead of frustrating—your customers.

Select Accomplishments:

• Increased customer satisfaction by 15% for a Fortune 500

• Reduced customer issue resolution time from 96 hours to 24 hours

• Streamlined processes to reduce annual overhead by $240K

If we have mutual interests, please send me an invitation to connect.

Expertise:

LEAN/Six Sigma, Process Mapping, Customer Experience (CX), Journey Mapping, Project Management

Voila! This example is short and sweet. If you're comfortable using the available 2,000 characters, you can share two to three stories that explain how you add value.

In summary: What → Why → How

What: Your headline showcasing what you do best.

Why: Opening statements in your summary to emphasize the value you bring and why it matters.

How: Your accomplishments or a story to support your opening summary statements.

Multiple approaches can be taken with your LinkedIn profile. This is simply one method. Remember, you have 2,000 characters (including spaces), but it's up to you how many you decide to use. Use the minimum number of characters needed to tell a compelling employer- or customer- focused story that illustrates what you do best that they need most.

I previously mentioned Donna Serdula, author of *LinkedIn Profile Optimization for Dummies* and the founder of LinkedIn-Makeover.com. I asked Donna to share some of her tips to create a compelling LinkedIn profile. You're in for a treat!

Crank Up Your Job Search with LinkedIn by Donna Serdula

Your LinkedIn profile is just your online resume. Simply copy and paste your resume into the fields of your LinkedIn profile and be done with it. Besides, who really cares anyway?

STOP. I did that too when I got on LinkedIn back in 2005. I leaned back and waited for opportunity to hit and nothing happened. But from that experience, I discovered a deep truth— your LinkedIn profile isn't your online resume. Your resume is your professional past; but your LinkedIn profile is your career future.

Your resume should align you with a particular job, whereas your LinkedIn profile is your first impression, digital introduction, and online reputation to the world. It should be your elevator pitch and your professional story. Your profile needs to be conversational and interesting, but most important, it needs to be written toward your goal and target audience.

Who Uses LinkedIn

Everyone who is anyone in hiring uses LinkedIn at some point. And why wouldn't they? LinkedIn is a database of professionals for professionals. That database is comprised of professional profiles that they themselves crafted (or copied and pasted).

Recruiters are often given a job description for a position they are hired to fill. They then use LinkedIn to find potential candidates who meet those qualifications. By performing searches on LinkedIn and stringing keywords together in a query, recruiters begin to narrow a list of candidates to those professionals who fit their target.

Hiring managers and HR professionals also use LinkedIn to learn more about candidates. Perhaps you submitted your resume to a company or applied to a job posting, and your resume stood out. That hiring manager or HR professional, intrigued by your resume, will search by name to find your LinkedIn profile, hoping to learn more about you.

Then let's say the recruiter requests your resume, you send it on, and it looks identical to what they just saw on your profile. BOTH are going to be disappointed, huh? In both instances, they wanted to learn more. Instead they got the same thing. That hiring manager might just assume that's all you offer and move on to another candidate.

The trick is to tell your professional story on LinkedIn and allow these two documents to build upon each other.

I'm not suggesting that your profile and resume are totally different but that the information on the resume and profile complement each other and provide additional information. The recruiter and hiring manager should come away intrigued, interested, and ready to contact you to learn more.

It's also important that you recognize that your LinkedIn profile is public. You don't want to share everything with everyone. Some accomplishments are better left to your resume and not stated in a public forum. "Saved current company from bankruptcy 3 times in the past 4 years" is not public fare.

How to Be Found

When recruiters are engaged to find the perfect job candidate, they are provided with a job description. The job description outlines the strengths and abilities the perfect candidate needs to possess. These strengths and abilities are keywords, and the recruiter will search not only his or her own database of resumes but will also search other databases like LinkedIn for those keywords in hopes of locating a pool of candidates that meet the job's requirements.

If you want to be found by a recruiter, you need to think like a recruiter and you must determine those keywords that define the perfect candidate of your desired position and inject these keywords into your profile. You will never get found for keywords that do not exist on your profile.

Think about your YouMap®— What are your strengths, values, and motivated skills? See how your YouMap® profile overlaps with your targeted job description. Utilize these words as your keywords.

Not only must you have the right keywords in your profile, you must also have a robust, strong network of first degree connections. The biggest misconception in the LinkedIn universe is how LinkedIn's search works. Most assume that when you search LinkedIn you are searching the entire database of users. This is true only if you are performing a name-based search OR paying for their premium recruiter corporate account (US$1,000 per month) for full access to the entire LinkedIn network.

Most users, and even most recruiters, who perform keyword-based searches are searching only their LinkedIn network. An individual's network is comprised of their first, second, and third degree connections and members of LinkedIn groups they belong to. So, if you want recruiters or hiring managers to find you (or if you want to find people) you need to make sure you have a large network. No one can find you if you are not in his or her network. If you want recruiters to find you, start connecting with recruiters.

I've found that most LinkedIn users are scared to accept people into their network or send invitations to people they don't know all that well. I don't advocate aiming low and wide to connect with everyone and their brother. Instead, make a strategic, conscious effort to connect with the right people. Then when a person sends you a connection request, accept if they look professional. You aren't connecting just to them, you are connecting to their connections and their connections' connections. That first-degree connection you are adding might not be in your industry, but people they know might be looking for someone just like you!

The Importance of Your LinkedIn Headline

I'm sure you've noticed it: the LinkedIn headline, that little tagline that sits at the top of everyone's LinkedIn profile. Sometimes, for some people, it looks interesting and eye-catching, but for most people it's just their title and current company.

When you first create your LinkedIn profile, your headline is simply taken from your current job title and company name. Because LinkedIn initially creates the headline for you, most people don't realize they can override this boring, default headline and add their own. In fact, most don't even realize how important the headline is.

The LinkedIn headline is one of the most under-utilized, yet most important parts, of your ENTIRE profile. What most people don't realize is that the LinkedIn headline isn't just statically located on the top of your profile. It moves throughout LinkedIn with you—defining you, introducing you, and potentially prompting people to want to learn more about YOU.

That 120-character tag line shows up on:

- Your LinkedIn search result listing
- Invitations to connect
- Connection suggestions
- Status updates
- LinkedIn messages
- Group discussions
- LinkedIn published articles
- Recommendations
- Who's Viewed Your Profile stats
- People You May Know section and more!

Because your headline is so visible, you want to make sure your LinkedIn headline communicates your value. When you are active on LinkedIn, that headline is often people's first impression of you, and it determines whether they read your profile or click to the next one.

Your headline also plays a big role in LinkedIn search results. It's no secret that when a person performs a keyword search in LinkedIn, profiles that contain those keywords in their headlines turn up higher in the search results. To enhance the likelihood that you will be found on LinkedIn, your headline should be chock-full of the keywords people are using to find someone like you.

Not only does the headline affect search results, it's a key component of the search result listings. When a recruiter performs a search on LinkedIn, they pore through the search results scanning profiles that match their search criteria. The search results listing is comprised of the person's profile picture, name, headline, location, potentially their current or a past position, and shared connections. The headline needs to catch that searcher's eye and compel him or her to click on your profile to learn more.

A successful headline concisely states who you are, what you do, and the benefit you bring to others. It should also contain the keywords people are using to find someone like you.

Start your headline with either your current job title or the job title of the position you are targeting. Then add your top keywords. Finish the headline with a benefit statement or uplifting message.

Here are a few examples:

Accomplished Client Services Manager ▶ Team Leader ▪ Saleforce.com Super User ▪ Enhancing Customer Satisfaction

Collections Specialist ▶ Negotiator ▪ Positive Rapport & Dispute Resolution ▪ Ensuring Timely Payments

Telesales Agent ✓ Cold Caller ✓ Prospecting ✓ Finding Profitable Business Relationships ✓ Exceeds Sales Targets

A successful headline should act like a welcoming beacon, directing people to view your profile. I know it's hard to come up with a headline on your own. If you need additional help, I created a free online application that walks you through creating a keyword-saturated headline. In less than ten clicks of your mouse, you'll have a compelling LinkedIn headline you can immediately copy and paste right into your LinkedIn profile. The generator even adds symbols to your headline automatically.

You can access this app here: http://www.linkedin-makeover.com/linkedin-headline-generator/

Creating an Impressive Summary

Congratulations, you have successfully directed and lured a recruiter or hiring manager to your profile. Now it's important to deliver the goods!

The LinkedIn Summary falls right below your name and headline and above the experience section. The summary area is where you introduce yourself to the reader. Your summary should be written in first person and should not be taken from your resume's professional summary paragraph. Don't succumb to the great temptation to write the summary in third person, writing as if you are telling a story about someone else, using pronouns like he, she, it or they. The problem with that narrative is that everyone knows it's your profile. Because you log in to your account and write your profile, third person voice is inauthentic and disingenuous. By writing in third person, you are not only creating distance between yourself and your reader, you clearly are not owning your story. Write in first person to draw in your reader and show you are a real person who takes pride in your work and ability. Claim your story and tell it proudly in your voice. Don't be afraid to use "I."

A successful summary tells your professional story succinctly and creates engagement between you and your reader. It is written toward your goal and target audience.

Whatever you do, stay away from resume speak. Write your summary in a natural, conversational manner. If you aren't sure, read it aloud to judge whether it sounds natural or stilted. Ultimately, the goal is for the readers to feel you are speaking to them directly, telling them exactly what they need to know about you.

State very clearly who you are and what you do. What are your core values? Once again, check out your YouMap® profile! Your YouMap® can help you determine what sets you apart. Also consider what results a person can expect from working with you. Why are you on LinkedIn? What are you trying to accomplish? What is your career vision? How did you get to this point in your career? Why do you do what you do? What motivates you? What is your career mission?

Take the time to make your summary your professional manifesto. By investing the time in writing your professional story, you are shaping your professional image into one that is high level, interesting, and attractive to recruiters and hiring managers.

Not sure what a great profile looks like? My company tweets out profiles we've optimized (unless our clients tell us to keep our work confidential). You can see examples of great profiles here: https://www.linkedin-makeover.com/linkedin-profile-examples/

Don't plagiarize but do look at these profiles as inspiration!

Splash Around

Taking the time to truly optimize your LinkedIn profile will yield opportunities far beyond what you would have attracted by simply copying and pasting your resume. Optimized profiles collide with more searches and appear in search results more often. They also have more profile views, get more invitations to connect, and receive more messages via LinkedIn.

Once you have an optimized profile and a strong LinkedIn network, the next step is to get active on LinkedIn. LinkedIn is more than just a bunch of profiles— it's a social network. The more active you are, the more LinkedIn will elevate your profile in search results. The more active you are the more people will see you and notice you. The more active you are the more opportunities will be presented to you. So how do you get active on LinkedIn?

First, start off by reading your LinkedIn feed. If you find it difficult to navigate to LinkedIn on your laptop or desktop computer, install the LinkedIn app on your phone. This way you don't have to make time for it. Instead, access it when you have time: waiting in line, through commercial breaks, on the train, before meetings, during boring meetings, while eating lunch, etc. Your LinkedIn feed is like a newspaper in which all the articles and posts were put together by your network of connections. It's a great way to stay on top of what's going on in your industry, community, and network.

Most people tend to get caught up in having to create content and become so paralyzed they do nothing. Rather than focusing on creating content, focus instead on curating content. If you are reading an interesting article, share it. Think of your LinkedIn's home page newsfeed as an online networking party where that tiny little status update is the virtual embodiment of a person standing in the middle of the room, looking for someone to talk to.

How do you want to respond to this person? If you simply want to smile and nod, click the Like button. If you want to engage and start a conversation, click the Comment button and type something pithy. If you want to promote this person and give them a bigger audience, click the Share button.

Success on LinkedIn comes when you have an optimized profile, a strong, robust network and activity; and engagement on the platform. Then when you find yourself with a new opportunity, that doesn't mean you shut down and disengage with LinkedIn. This professional platform isn't just for job searching. It's a place to network, forge relationships, help others, educate, add value, and inspire. Keep adding to your network, stay engaged, and add value, and you will never again have to find a job. Jobs will find you!

For more in-depth self-help for LinkedIn, you can pick up a copy of

LinkedIn Profile Optimization for Dummies or visit LinkedIn-Makeover.com to work with Donna's team of professional LinkedIn profile writers.

You might be wondering how to tackle some of the other sections of your LinkedIn profile. Lisa Jones will wrap up the section on LinkedIn to touch on some basics of other relevant LinkedIn profile sections.

Supplementary LinkedIn Sections by Lisa Jones

Many hiring managers and recruiters will tell you that having a LinkedIn profile is a must, and this is advice I strongly agree with. As Donna pointed out, an online presence is vital, regardless of whether you are looking for a new job or seeking stronger professional visibility to manage your career.

Creating a LinkedIn profile and using it to successfully network with other professionals will provide a more effective way to start conversations with those who are able to hire you or will refer you to someone who can. Many recruiters and hiring managers spend a large amount of time on LinkedIn, which makes social networking a must.

As with your resume, your LinkedIn profile needs to be positioned, branded, and aligned with your career objectives. It's important to make your profile distinctive and appealing to your audience and, as Donna also stressed, not a copy-and-paste of your resume.

LinkedIn profiles are much more than a resume because you have more available space to add content along with the ability to add media such as slides, videos, and graphics. When writing a resume, it's best to write in short, concise sentences leaving out pronouns and articles. However, when writing an LI profile, you can show your personality to draw people in to read more about you and the kind of work environment where you will excel.

Even though Applicant Tracking Systems will not be reading your LinkedIn profile, keywords are essential because they are an integral part of how people search for you. I don't agree with keyword "stuffing" and implore you to use keywords in a contextual way when writing accomplishment statements to demonstrate your knowledge, skills, and abilities.

Keywords are especially important in LinkedIn profile headlines and should be positioned for viewing on a mobile device as well as a desktop computer. (Log into your LinkedIn profile from both your mobile and desktop to see how your headline displays after you update it). I also suggest focusing on adding "hard" skills to the headline to shape how you want to be perceived.

For example:

Senior Accounts Manager | Territory Management | 15+ Years
Leading Business Development & Channel Management | Fortune 500

Tip: Use the headline to showcase what is most important and relevant about you and your career goals. Showcase motivated transferable skills identified in your YouMap®. Use synonyms for skills commonly found in job descriptions. For example, "Logistics" might be more industry appropriate than "Make Arrangements."

Remember, the Summary section of a LinkedIn profile provides 2,000 characters and is the best place to be creative with the information you include. You can add links to websites, podcasts, and other multimedia tools. However, it is most important to focus on information that clearly communicates the value you will bring to an organization.

I also suggest adding keywords (skills) in each section of your profile that are relevant to your career goals to break up large blocks of text for easier readability and a more visually appealing profile.

Tip: Make sure any graphics uploaded to your profile are clear quality or this will detract from professionalism and may cause readers to move on to other candidates. Also, LinkedIn currently limits your photo file size to 8MB.

Following are the additional LinkedIn sections, beyond the headline and summary, that I recommend you take time to complete.

Experience

This section is where you showcase your work history. As with your resume, do not write out your job description. Instead, write a brief paragraph to summarize the value you bring (or brought) to an organization based on the role you are seeking.

A brief paragraph followed by accomplishment statements is the best format to use, starting with your most current, high impact statements. Write your accomplishment statements by explaining the challenges you faced and how you overcame each challenge.

> **Tip:** Avoid paragraphs longer than five lines and keep accomplishment statements (bullets) to only two lines. You will lose your reader if they must read lengthy paragraphs.

Start with your most current job and follow the advice in the resume writing section. No one wants to read information that is not relevant to your career path. Choose your most relevant accomplishments. Remember, transferable skills are important if you are changing careers.

Education

List your most current education. Never list your high school unless you did not pursue further education. However, if you have been out of high school for at least five years, leave it off.

Volunteer Experience

Establishing yourself within your professional community on a local and national level is important to achieving long-term career success and credibility. Listing volunteer work is as important for those who are job seeking as for career management.

Many career services professionals caution against including outdated community service that does not serve your current career interests. While you might choose to feature transferable experience from the distant past, when it comes to volunteering, this does not typically apply.

Using a 5-year rule is a great starting place when considering what to include in the volunteer section of your profile. Volunteer experience older than five years should relate to your next desired job. Improve the volunteer section by listing the name of organizations you have volunteered with and including the corporate logo, if available. When you add the organization name, LinkedIn will pre-populate the logo if the organization has a LinkedIn company page.

Tip: LinkedIn gives you the option (as with other sections) to choose a beginning and end date. If you are currently volunteering with an organization, select the "I currently volunteer here" checkbox.

Accomplishments

The accomplishments section is the place to list your publications, certifications, patents, courses, projects, honors and awards, and test scores.

Tip: The five-year rule should be used with caution here. When I work with IT professionals, we exclude more technology certifications and capabilities than we keep. New certifications supersede old ones. Keep only those certifications relevant to your audience. Due to rapid technology changes, some information may be out of date and/or irrelevant to the career path you have chosen. However, always remember that age and relevance are not synonymous. If it matters, include it. If it doesn't matter, exclude it.

Skills and Endorsements

LinkedIn allows you to add fifty skills to your profile. This is where you can showcase your motivated transferable skills. Your contacts can endorse you for skills. Therefore, avoid adding skills that are irrelevant to your chosen path. You want your contacts to endorse you for skills you want to be known for.

Tip: Skills can be moved and reordered to draw a reader's attention to the most important skills. To move a skill, click the edit pencil in the upper right corner. Then, click on the four stacked horizontal lines to the right of the skill and drag it up or down.

Regular LinkedIn profile maintenance is key, just as with your resume. Make your profile clear and targeted to the job you are seeking. If you appear unsure of what you are looking for, a recruiter or hiring manager will be unsure of your capabilities and knowledge. Keep it relevant and keep your profile updated.

Finally, remember to network and to nurture your network connections after you have "linked up." It's important to not only network with hiring managers and recruiters but to also network with those in professional associations and community and alumni networks.

Now, it's time for me (Kristin) to take back the reigns and shift from job search materials to interview strategy!

How to Wow Interviewers

The focus of this interview section is to help you showcase what you do best and connect that to what the employer needs most in a job interview. According to Jobvite, failure to differentiate yourself—in other words stand out—is one of the top reasons for not receiving a job offer.

Because the specific focus of Show the World! is telling your story in a way that makes you stand out, I will not cover interview topics such as overcoming nerves, how to answer trick questions, salary negotiation, and so forth. For a comprehensive interview resource that covers those topics and many more, you can pick up a copy of my interview preparation book, *5 Surprising Steps to Land the Job NOW!*

Preparing for the Interview

For your upcoming interview, you'll want to cross-reference your YouMap® to the job description and write down success stories to create a bridge between what you offer and what the employer needs through real-life examples.

Highlight key words and phrases in the job description that indicate what the company seeks in a candidate, such as skills, experiences, personality, and character traits.

Next, create a chart following these steps:

- List requirements you highlighted on the job description in the Employer Need column.
- List skills, traits, strengths, and values you've captured in your YouMap® under What I do Best, in addition to any related experience.
- Write a brief results-focused story to substantiate what you do best under Tell My Story.

An example is shown below.

EMPLOYER NEED	WHAT I DO BEST	TELL MY STORY
Improve systems, processes, policies	-Have improved 12 processes in current role in the past year.	I have improved processes in every role in the past 10 years. In my current position, I have made 12 process improvements in the past year, including moving from a manual spreadsheet process for our client pricing to a web-based system, which has increased my team's profitability by 25%.
Long term planning	-4 years strategic planning exp. at ACME -Strategic thinking is a top five strength in StrengthsFinder	In my current role as an Operations Manager, I have been directly involved in program strategic planning for three consecutive years. The annual planning process includes program growth strategy, associate learning and development strategy, customer experience and retention strategy, and business process innovation. We have experienced financial growth year-over-year, as well as low employee turnover of less than 5%, and 15% growth of our new customer base and a 25% increase in existing customer sales.

Payroll management	No experience	While I have not had direct experience w/payroll, I have Learner in my top five strengths, which means I learn new things very quickly. For example, I managed a $3M budgetary process independently within two weeks with no prior budgeting experience. Given budget development is a more complex process than payroll, I am confident I would learn the process equally as quickly, if not faster.

By completing this mapping exercise, you will be equipped and prepared with solid stories linked directly to the requirements taken from the job description. When asked, "What can you do for us?" and "Why should we hire you?" you'll have these answers in the bag if you map yourself to the job description using the above technique.

Why Do You Want to Work Here?

Research, research, research the company and be prepared to connect your values to the values of the organization. What is it about the culture that makes you a good fit? I talked about this previously in "Targeting Opportunities" and "Cover Letter Basics," so you are well on your way to nailing this question.

How many times have you heard someone wasn't selected for a job or was let go because, "It just wasn't a good fit"? My friend, Caroline, shared recently that she memorized a company's mission statement and incorporated it into her answer to "Why do you want to work here?" She got the job!

The more you know about the company, the better you'll be able to determine if you are a good fit for their culture and be able to tell them why you are.

Tell Me About Yourself

At the beginning of an interview, an interviewer will often invite you to tell him or her about yourself. The most common way people answer this question is with an overview of their work history:

"I graduated in 2005 from UNC Chapel Hill with a degree in computer science and a minor in business. After graduating, I went to work for Microsoft as a business analyst on the Microsoft Office team. I was promoted to senior business analyst after eighteen months and then moved to the ASP.NET team."

Boring. Predictable. Unmemorable.

These work history speeches don't reveal anything new or interesting about you and are simply a dreary recap of your resume. "Tell me about yourself" is a great opportunity to stand out from the competition and demonstrate a clear picture of what you do best that the employer needs. This is another instance where you can put your YouMap® to great use.

Print a copy of your one-page YouMap® for each person you'll be meeting in the interview. When you're invited to "Tell me about yourself," give them each a copy and draw their attention to the My Unique Contribution statement. Share your unique contribution and tell them a brief twenty-to-sixty second success story to back it up. Explain you've invested a lot of time to really know who you are and the value you will bring them. What do you think the statistical chances are the other candidates will do this?

Example:

> "The best way to describe myself is by sharing this summary with you. I have a reputation of generating innovative ideas that haven't been considered. For example, last year I was responsible for the launch of a new injection therapy, but physicians were resistant to the new protocol.
>
> I had to figure out a way to make it easier for the doctors to use, so I collaborated with the hospital to innovate and influence hospital protocol. As a result, the process was streamlined, physicians began prescribing the new drug,

> patients had a better experience, and I increased my sales by 210% over the prior year.
>
> This kind of innovation best characterizes a common thread in my career: I enjoy finding better, more effective ways of doing things. That's me in a nutshell."

In this example above, the second sentence is the person's unique contribution statement, and the rest is the evidence to prove it. If you aren't offered the tell me about yourself opening, you will have other opportunities to share your YouMap® in the interview, such as this question...

What are Your Strengths?

If you've already provided a copy of your YouMap® to the interviewer, you can direct their attention to the "My Strengths" section to address this question. If not, this question is a great time to provide the interviewer with a copy.

> **Tip**: You might be interviewing for a promotion in your current company, where handing over a YouMap® won't make sense for your culture. Even without giving interviewers a physical copy of the YouMap®, you will still be better prepared to execute on your approach having gone through the process.

The first video of my YouTube vlog, Career Wisdom Walk, outlines a completely unique strategy to explain your strengths in a job interview. If you can't access the link below, you can simply enter "Kristin Sherry" or "Career Wisdom Walk" within YouTube's search to find my channel. The video is titled, "How to answer, 'What are your strengths?': E1 Career Wisdom Walk."

Here is a link to the video: tinyurl.com/yd4stnmc

You will get more depth from watching the video, but in summary, here are the steps:

1. Underline phrases that describe you best in your downloaded "Strengths Insight Guide" from Gallup. See the "Discover Your Strengths" section of this book for details if you haven't taken the Clifton StrengthsFinder assessment yet.

2. Open your word processing program and either paste the definition for each of your five strengths as well as the sentence that best describes you from your "Strengths Insight Guide," or simply paste two or three descriptive sentences. The definitions of the strengths are optional.

3. Print and take a copy of this single page (do not exceed one page) to the interview for each person you will meet. Bring an additional copy for yourself and a couple of spares for unexpected interviewers.

4. When asked your strengths, provide each interviewer with a copy and explain you've taken a strengths assessment and brought your results to share.

5. Connect one of your strengths to the job by mentioning a requirement you saw in the job description related to your strength and tell a success (S.T.A.R) story illustrating the use of this strength.

Here is an example of what your handout might look like:

Jane Doe Strengths Summary

Input

Inquisitive, curious, researcher, open, and absorb information. I utilize information that I collect to inform, teach and support other people.

Learner

A desire to learn and continuously improve. Dynamic learner. When I enter a new environment or situation, I am able to get up to speed quickly on how things work.

Arranger

I excel in times of chaos and I am the calm in the storm. Strong at coordinating all the moving parts to maximize productivity. Reputation for accomplishing whatever needs to be done. Seek complex, dynamic work environments.

Individualization

Intrigued by the unique qualities of each person. Attentive to people's individual style, attitudes, and interests. Able to customize my approach.

Communication

Able to take charge, speak up and be heard with internal and external stakeholders. Collaborative. Enjoy sharing ideas, exchanging information, and trading stories. Able to explain complex information in a simple manner. Good conversationalist and presenter.

If you feel comfortable explaining your StrengthsFinder themes, you don't need to bring a separate printout of your strengths; simply refer the interviewer back to your YouMap® where your five strengths are listed. I suggest the separate sheet with the phrases describing your strengths to help facilitate a conversation with the interviewer if you're not yet comfortable describing your strengths without a visual aid.

What is Your Greatest Weakness?

You might be surprised that after all my focus on what makes you a unique masterpiece that I would include a question focusing on weaknesses. I chose to do so because our greatest weakness, oftentimes, can be overuse of a strength. Also, discussing your weakness gives you another opportunity to reinforce one of your strengths, even if you sometimes over use it.

I've listed the thirty-four strengths below, along with the potential barriers people might see if we are overusing our strengths.

Locate each of your Top 5 strengths in the list and identify which of the barriers might be true of you in the last column.

STRENGTH	POSITIVES PEOPLE MIGHT SEE	BARRIERS PEOPLE MIGHT SEE
ACTIVATOR	No substitute for action; do it until you get it right	Leaps before looking
ACHIEVER	Wants to get it done; intense diligence	Work is more important than people
ADAPTABILITY	Likes change and variety; responds well to change	Appears directionless
ANALYTICAL	Truth is objective and must be measured	Analysis paralysis
ARRANGER	Multiplicity; juggler who touches all the balls	Difficult to follow; frequent rearrangements
BELIEF	Only one right way—will not be distracted; seeing comes with believing	Set in ways

COMMAND	Creates clarity through polarization; people drawn to you because they know what you think	Bossy, dictator
COMMUNICATION	Thinks and learns best when talking with others; telling a story helps others understand better	Blabbermouth
COMPETITION	Better performance via watching others; scoreboard measures your progress and validates victory	Sore loser
CONNECTEDNESS	Accepts mystery; aware of inherent, invisible unity that already exists	Flaky, new-ager, not in touch with reality
CONSISTENCY	Treating everyone the same; promotes fairness	Rules trump relationships and results

CONTEXT	Remembers and reveres what has been; can go forward after understanding the history	Stuck in the past
DELIBERATIVE	Anticipates obstacles; plans for the unexpected	Hesitant; slows things down; socially cautious
DEVELOPER	Notices/promotes growth in others; natural mentor and coach	Wastes time on low performers
DISCIPLINE	Feels good to meet deadlines; creates structure and order	Might be resistant to change; seen as inflexible
EMPATHY	Knows how others are feeling; relies on intuition	Bleeding heart
FOCUS	Identifies priorities quickly; goal-setter, goal-getter	Destination mentality could limit enjoyment of the journey

FUTURISTIC	Visionary, clear picture of the future you want to build	Head in the clouds
HARMONY	Can find common ground; looks for consensus	Afraid of conflict
IDEATION	Improves on the existing, sees connections others miss	Impractical, lacks follow-through
INCLUDER	Works for acceptance of those on outside, accepting of everyone	Indiscriminate; generous to a fault
INDIVIDUALIZATION	Appreciates differences; finds the right job for each person	Sacrifices group need for individual needs
INPUT	Collects things potentially helpful; helps by sharing tangible tools	Pack rat with too much lying around

INTELLECTION	Inquiring approach to growth and learning; thinks about concepts that need understanding	Isolated and aloof
LEARNER	Interests guide intentions; always interested in learning something new	Curiosity might lead to irrelevance or nonproductivity
MAXIMIZER	Aspires to meet/exceed standard of excellence; wants to build something great	Picky, never satisfied
POSITIVITY	Light-hearted; generous with praise	Naive
RELATOR	Genuine, authentic; can make a connection with almost anyone	Cliquish, plays favorites/inner circle
RESPONSIBILITY	Does things right, does the right thing, do what I say I will	Can't say no or let go

RESTORATIVE	Troubleshooter; finds improvements and solutions	Perceived as negative or critical, always pointing out problems
SELF-ASSURANCE	Strong inner compass; certain, willing to take risks	Arrogant, overly confident, self-sufficient
SIGNIFICANCE	Does things of importance; desires to be seen and heard	Attention hound, showboat
STRATEGIC	Determines most viable options; good judgment; identifies risks	Naysayer
WOO	Builds broad social network, winning others over	Phony, superficial

Tips:
- Do not provide an example story or elaborate on your weakness unless asked. Stories make your weakness memorable. If asked, share what you've learned or have attempted to improve.
- Stay positive; avoid weaknesses that are important requirements for the job. For example, for a customer service role, do not share that you're critical, impatient, inflexible, lack follow-through, or put work ahead of people.
- Avoid sharing a weakness you haven't attempted to improve.

- Avoid interpersonal weaknesses unless you can demonstrate you've made significant improvement. This would be an instance where a story is acceptable and encouraged.
- Share what you did to take ownership and act, and how you applied it as a learning experience for the future. Most of your talk time is spent here, not on the weakness itself.

Reflect on your greatest weakness and write out a brief characterization in the space provided.

_____

_____

_____

_____

_____

_____

_____

_____

_____

_____

Storytelling with S.T.A.R.

Again, S.T.A.R. is an acronym for Situation, Task, Action, and Result. S.T.A.R. stories are used to answer behavior-based inquiries that begin, "Tell me about a time when... ."

As a hiring manager, I was surprised how often people answered a specific behavior-based question with a general response. For example, when I was an operations manager interviewing for an open role on my team, I asked, "What does integrity mean to you? And tell me about a time you demonstrated integrity at work."

The candidate proceeded to share that integrity is doing the right thing, even when no one is looking (so far, so good), but then she continued sharing a general self-assessment about her commitment to always do the right thing and go above and beyond. Nowhere in her answer did she share a specific example of when she demonstrated integrity on the job.

When asked a behavior-based question, remember to avoid present-tense generalizations such as, "I always... ." Talk is cheap, and anyone can say what an interviewer wants to hear or what they think they would do in a theoretical situation. The hiring manager wants to hear what you did in a real situation. Prove it with the S.T.A.R. format!

As you review your YouMap®, think of several S.T.A.R. stories to illustrate some of the insights about yourself to an interviewer—especially your strengths. The downloadable Strengths Worksheet is the best place to capture stories for your interview. Download the strengths worksheet at MyYouMap.com.

Your story should be between twenty seconds and two minutes in length. Be brief and let the interviewer know you'd be happy to go into greater detail if needed. This prevents you from eating up too much of your interview time with stories the interviewer is less interested in and allows you to expand upon stories they are most interested in.

Situation

What was the problem or opportunity you faced? Provide a brief background. I can't emphasize enough the importance of brevity! You might be tempted to share every detail. Please don't!

An interviewer needs only enough context to grasp and understand the significance of the RESULT. The result is the most important part of your story, yet many interviewees begin rambling about the situation and sharing unnecessary details the employer cares little about.

Task

How did you address the problem or opportunity you faced? In other words, what was the end goal? Again, keep this brief.

Action

What specific actions did you take? What was your involvement? How did you contribute? In short, what did you do? Don't dig into the gory details of every step. What label can you give what you did to convey meaning without a lengthy explanation of all the steps?

For example, "I performed a root cause analysis" or "I developed a detailed project plan" conveys a lot of meaning, which eliminates the need to describe each step you performed in detail.

Result

The result is the outcome of your action and the most important part of the story. How did you make a difference? Did you save the company time, money, or other resources? Did someone get a promotion because of your investment in them? Did you increase efficiencies? Did you do something that hadn't been thought of or tried before?

Providing context of why the result mattered is important. Interviewers don't know why your outcome is a big deal, so you'll need to help them understand. Let's look at an example.

> *Employer:* What is an accomplishment you're proud of?
>
> *Interviewee:* Last year I was selected to join the company's leadership development program.

As an interviewer, my first question is, "So what?" This is not a high impact statement because no context is provided.

Was this program exclusive, or are 90 percent of employees given the same opportunity? How many others were selected? Out of how many? Did you have to be nominated, versus applying for yourself?

Let's look at a more effective response.

> *Interviewee:* Recently, I was nominated by a senior leader in the company to participate in a high potential leadership program. Two-hundred sixty-four employees were nominated, and I was one of only five people selected.

Here's another example:

> *Interviewer:* Tell me about a recent success.
>
> *Interviewee:* Last year I managed a shared services integration project with a positive process and financial outcome.

This is an actual example from a client. Were they selected for the project? Was it enterprise-wide, or a small project? How complex was the project? Was it a high visibility project?

Sometimes you might not have numbers if you didn't take them with you from your last job. It's OK if you don't have them. You can characterize your success using words. Let's look at where this accomplishment ended up after I asked my client these questions.

> *Interviewee:* I was appointed as the program manager to oversee five project managers on a highly confidential, business-critical shared services integration for a Fortune 100 company, which finished on time and within budget and resulted in a stronger financial position for the company.

Ask the Right Questions

Another great way to use your YouMap® is the deal makers and deal breakers I asked you to highlight at the end of the "Find Yourself" section. Your criteria of what must be both present and absent for your next career move is an important source for creating questions to ask an interviewer.

Remember, you are interviewing a company as much as they are interviewing you.

In my experience, your values are a significantly important source for interview questions, because values violations are a top cause of job dissatisfaction. For example, people who value growth, accomplishment, results, and making a difference are very unsatisfied in roles where they're not stretched or contributing something that matters to them.

Those who value autonomy feel stifled in roles where they aren't allowed to make decisions or are too closely managed. Perhaps you'll want to also ask a question to discover what a typical day might look like in the role to ensure your strengths and motivating skills are used.

Your "must have" and "must avoid" conditions help you make more informed choices when presented with an offer. Prioritize your top two deal makers and deal breakers to generate four questions to ask in the interview. Here are sample questions based on hypothetical values for an individual's next role:

Value/Need: A manager who's interested in growing and developing his or her team

Question: Can you share how you've directly contributed to a team member's career growth in the past six-to-twelve months?

Value/Need: Freedom of autonomous decision-making

Question: How do prefer your team members to manage problem solving and decision making related to their work, and can you provide a recent example?

Value/Need: A collaborative work environment

Question: How would you describe the working dynamic of this team? What are some things you've done to build a more collaborative team culture?

Value/Need: Learning new skills

> **Question:** Could you share some of the learning and training opportunities you and your team have been given in the past year.
>
> **Value/Need:** Current technology and tools to do my job effectively
>
> **Question:** What kind of tools will be provided to the person who enters this role?

In summary, prepare for an interview by:

- Generating stories about what you do best that the employer needs most.
- Learning to clearly and confidently tell interviewers about yourself by sharing one of the following: your strengths, values, motivating skills, or how your career interests are wired. Connect it back to what the interviewer is looking for in the job description.
- Thoughtfully determine the best questions to ask an interviewer based on your deal makers and deal breakers.

These steps will equip you to more effectively evaluate the role, manager, and workplace culture fit.

Asking the right questions will provide you with heightened discernment to accept a role that's right for you and the courage to turn down a role that isn't, leading to better job fit for the rest of your life.

Final Thoughts

In your quest to explore, discover, and learn new skills to display your gifting to the world, I am deeply honored you chose me as one of your guides.

My sincere hope is that you carry what you've learned about yourself throughout your life, that you are true to yourself, and that going forward you are better equipped to love Mondays!

Always remember your conditions of career satisfaction. Revisit your values, motivating skills, strengths, and interests throughout your life. Let your brilliance shine. Be you. You are a masterpiece, and I'm rooting for you!

"Caged Bird" by Maya Angelou
A free bird leaps
on the back of the wind
and floats downstream
till the current ends
and dips his wing
in the orange sun rays
and dares to claim the sky.

But a bird that stalks
down his narrow cage
can seldom see through
his bars of rage
his wings are clipped and
his feet are tied
so he opens his throat to sing.

The caged bird sings
with a fearful trill
of things unknown
but longed for still

and his tune is heard
on the distant hill
for the caged bird
sings of freedom.

The free bird thinks of another breeze
and the trade winds soft through the sighing trees
and the fat worms waiting on a dawn bright lawn
and he names the sky his own.

But a caged bird stands on the grave of dreams
his shadow shouts on a nightmare scream
his wings are clipped and his feet are tied
so he opens his throat to sing.

The caged bird sings
with a fearful trill
of things unknown
but longed for still
and his tune is heard
on the distant hill
for the caged bird
sings of freedom.

About the Author

KRISTIN SHERRY is a career consultant, author, speaker, and founder of Virtus Career Consulting. She helps people love Mondays through five areas of focus: coach certifications, individual career discovery coaching, executive coaching, workshops and speaking, and writing.

She is one of only twenty consultants world-wide certified as a Master Trainer in the WorkPlace Big Five Profile™, a human resource optimization and workforce development tool used by more than eight thousand organizations across forty-eight countries.

As a Learning & Development leader at a Fortune 20 company, Kristin managed the company's learning strategy and coached leaders and their teams.

Her career discovery and empowerment book, *Follow Your Star: Career Lessons I Learned from Mom*, and interviewing book, *5 Surprising Steps to Land the Job NOW!*, were released in 2016 and 2017, respectively. Kristin is a member of The Authors Guild and has been featured in numerous print, radio and podcast interviews; articles; and blogs read by millions of people in dozens of countries.

Kristin speaks on career topics in forums such as the National Career Thought Leader Conference and facilitates quarterly career workshops in the Charlotte, NC, area. She lives in North Carolina with her husband Xander and their children.

Want to Work with Kristin?

SPEAKING:
Kristin speaks on career and leadership topics such as:
- Finding Career Fulfillment
- Career Management
- Work/Life Prioritization
- Leadership Development
- Increasing Communication Power & Influence
- Interpersonal Skills & Productive Conflict
- Workplace Culture

WORKSHOPS & TRAINING:
- Get certified as a YouMap® Coach
- Get certified as a YouMap® Workshop Facilitator
- Get certified as a WorkPlace Big Five Profile™ Consultant
- Discover Your Strengths Workshop (StrengthsFinder)
- Building Better Relationships Workshop (DiSC®)
- Creating High Impact Teams Workshop
- Productive Conflict Workshop

CONSULTING:
YouMap® Consultations, Adult and Student Career Exploration, Career Transition, Career Management, Leadership Development and Executing Coaching.

Contact us to share your career goals and explore how we can help you reach them. We consult with individuals and organizations.

MEDIA:
Interview Kristin for your radio or TV show, podcast, or print media. She will deliver fresh insights with practical application for your audience.

Contact Stephanie Hall: stephanie@virtuscareers.com

Follow Kristin on Social Media!

LinkedIn: www.linkedin.com/in/kristinsherry

Virtus Career Consulting: www.linkedin.com/company/9405586/

Facebook: www.facebook.com/virtuscareers

Instagram: @virtuscareers

Twitter: @Virtus_Careers

YouTube "Career Wisdom Walk" Vlog: tinyurl.com/ybdktta7

Tools & Resources

Readers should be aware that internet sites mentioned as references or sources might have changed or no longer be available.

Other Books by Kristin Sherry

5 Surprising Steps to Land the Job NOW! – tinyurl.com/ybt9fsm5

Follow Your Star: Career Lessons I Learned from Mom – tinyurl.com/ydera8fg

Downloads

Download book resources at MyYouMap.com:

-Coachee Strengths Worksheet
-Values Exercise
-Motivated Skills Exercise
-YouMap® Career Profile Template
-Networking Sheet
-Career Decision-Making Tool

Websites

StrengthsFinder Assessment: tinyurl.com/yar7d7f4
LinkedIn Headline Generator: http://www.linkedin-makeover.com/linkedin-headline-generator/
Education Credential Equivalency
    Canada: tinyurl.com/ya952klw
    US: tinyurl.com/y98epfws
O*NET Online: www.onetonline.org
My Next Move Career Interest Profiler
    Military Veteran Career Interest Profiler: www.mynextmove.org/vets/
    Standard Career Interest Profiler: www.mynextmove.org/explore/ip
    Spanish Language Career Interest Profiler: www.miproximopaso.org/

What's Next?

Learn to manage your career with Paul Carney's book, *Move Your Æ: Know, Grow, and Show Your Career Value*. Available on Amazon.

Resume & LinkedIn Profile Writers

PATRICIA EDWARDS has spent her entire career, more than 25 years, recruiting, interviewing, hiring and developing professionals in her role as Senior Human Resources and Talent Manager for Fortune 100 and 200 companies. She estimates she has reviewed more than 40,000 resumes, interviewed 3,000 and hired more than 1,000 people in financial services, healthcare, sales, customer service, and not-for-profit organizations.

Several years ago, she discovered her gift and passion is educating, empowering, and inspiring people to attain their ideal career. She has coached hundreds of employees, at all levels, to their career success and now shares her career wisdom with job seekers from new grads starting out their careers to mid-career professionals seeking a career change and to those in the C-Suite.

Patricia knows what it takes to get hired and promoted because she has made those decisions on behalf of organizations and guides her clients through a job search strategy process including personal branding, resume renovation, LinkedIn strategy building, and interview coaching. She holds a degree from Iowa State University, has completed graduate work toward an MBA, a Master's degree in organizational development, and is a Certified Facilitator/Trainer of Emotional Intelligence.

Contact Patricia:

patricia@careerwisdomcoach.com | linkedin.com/in/patriciaedwardscareercoach

KERRI TWIGG is an international career consultant who helps people use and confidently share their stories. She has worked with hundreds of people to create resumes and job search strategies that land her clients their ideal jobs. And, if they don't know what kind of job, she helps with that too.

Kerri is a strategist, and her clients benefit from her more than fifteen years of experience as a workshop facilitator and career transition consultant. Kerri's career started in the arts where she worked as a drama instructor and playwright, both of which inform her coaching methods. She helps clients find their career story and share it with impact on paper and in person. Most of her clients compliment and appreciate her approachable and practical coaching style that they say leaves them feeling confident about their value and values in the workplace. Clients say her coaching advice lasts beyond the job search to positively influence how they present themselves to others past the job interview.

Kerri is a Certified Resume Strategist and holds a BA in theatre and a Master's degree in humane education. Her ideal clients work in industries that don't harm people, animals or the environment. Kerri uses a heart-centered and stories style, and her clients often land jobs at 15-40% higher pay using their favorite skills. Kerri has worked with professionals from almost every sector ranging from bakers to robotics engineers. She is an energetic keynote speaker and has taught in boardrooms, schools, theaters, and even a boathouse. She writes and shares career resources at career-stories.com.

Contact Kerri: kerri@career-stories.com | linkedin.com/in/kerritwigg

KAMARA TOFFOLO is a resume writer, LinkedIn consultant, and job search strategist who helps her clients DARE to do work differently! Whether a bold and brazen professional ready to shake things up and make a big career change, a go-getting manager primed to score a well-deserved promotion, or a high-impact executive strategizing their next career transition, Kamara helps her clients land great-fitting gigs!

Serving clients globally, Kamara has worked with high-achieving professionals from Canada, USA, UK, Australia, Japan, India, UAE, and Brazil, to name a few.

She is a "career storyteller." Kamara takes her clients' unique career stories and crafts a compelling resume and LinkedIn profile that highlights their strengths and accomplishments while honoring their authentic journeys. After working with Kamara, her clients get interviews in a matter of weeks.

A trusted job searching expert, Kamara has been a featured writer and contributor to many publications including Forbes, Business Insider, Inc., and The Daily Muse, among others.

Prior to making her mark in career development, Kamara spent twelve years in the financial services and technology industries working for corporations from small and medium-sized businesses to Fortune 500 companies. She is an Erickson Certified Professional Coach and holds a Bachelor of Commerce degree in entrepreneurial management.

When not working her resume and LinkedIn magic, Kamara shares her insight speaking at professional conferences, seminars, and universities and delivers custom corporate workshops and training.

Kamara is based in Ottawa, but originally is from Vancouver. She enjoys time with her husband Paul and cat Bart. In her spare time, she studies improv comedy and foreign languages and enjoys travel and Judd Apatow movies.

Contact Kamara: kamara@kamaratoffolo.com | linkedin.com/in/kamarat

LISA JONES is a resume and academic CV writer, LinkedIn writer, career strategist, and founder of Specialized Resume Services. Through her prior work experience and academic background, Lisa can write for all levels of job seekers worldwide. On a personal level, Lisa has a passion for helping job seekers and not only provides a resume or CV but also teaches her clients why she writes documents as she does and helps them find the resources they need to become successful. Lisa's strength is breaking down complex career-related information in a way that all job seekers can understand.

She also has a strong academic background with a Master of Business Administration and serves as an alumni mentor for the University of Phoenix. Lisa holds an Executive Certificate in Human Resources from Cornell, an Executive Certificate in Applied Business Strategies from Notre Dame.

Lisa started her career with one of the largest printing ink manufacturers in the world. During this time, she held many positions including purchasing, inventory control, logistics, human resources, and technical sales. During her corporate career, Lisa hired and trained many personnel and worked with engineers, marketers, scientists, C-Level executives, and owners of companies. This experience has given hands-on knowledge of many jobs and the ability to work with a wide range of clients.

Contact Lisa: lisa_a_jones@msn.com | linkedin.com/in/lisajonessrs

DONNA SERDULA pioneered the concept of LinkedIn profile optimization, realizing early on that the LinkedIn profile was much more than just an online resume. The LinkedIn profile is an amazing opportunity for branding.

Donna spent the first ten years of her career in sales, marketing, and training. She joined LinkedIn's social network in 2005 and promptly copied and pasted her resume then wondered what all the fuss was about. A job change in 2006 led her back to LinkedIn as she looked for tools to help her build a sales territory. During this time, she had her LinkedIn epiphany and forged her LinkedIn profile methodology. By integrating LinkedIn into her sales process, she found amazing success.

In 2009, she walked away from her successful sales career and founded Vision Board Media and LinkedIn-Makeover.com. Her mission: To help people realize their Internet identity and shape an identity that makes an impact and leads to opportunity.

From that day on, Donna Serdula became a chief influencer, advocating and evangelizing the importance of taking control of your Internet identity. By presenting yourself in a way that inspires and builds confidence in your abilities, products, and services, you are shaping your future.

As the foremost expert in LinkedIn profile optimization, she's proven that a strong LinkedIn profile is the key to performing well on LinkedIn. Through her website LinkedIn-Makeover.com, Donna and her team of more than thirty writers have helped more than five thousand executives, entrepreneurs, professionals, and companies from all over the world tell their unique stories and brand themselves successfully.

Donna is an in-demand speaker throughout the US, and she has been featured on Business Insider, Time's Money Magazine, Wall Street Journal's Market Watch, LA Times, NBC, SiriusXM Radio's "The Focus Group," and many other news outlets.

Contact Donna: donna@linkedin-makeover.com | linkedin.com/in/todonna

Thank you so much for reading one of our **Business** books.
If you enjoyed our book, please check out our recommended title for your next great read!

BEST by James E. Russell III

"This is a new view into how to look for as well as to be the best." –Tara Rixey, Account Manager/Recruiter, *Hire the Winners*

View other Black Rose Writing titles at www.blackrosewriting.com/books

and use promo code **PRINT** to receive a **20% discount** when purchasing

Made in the USA
Middletown, DE
19 June 2019